The Magic of the Swatchways

THE MAGIC HOUR

THE MAGIC OF THE SWATCHWAYS

CAMEOS OF CRUISING IN SMALL YACHTS

By

Maurice Griffiths

Author of "Yachting on a Small Income"

Illustrated by
F. B. Harnack

NAUTICAL

Reproduced and printed in Gt. Britain by
Whitstable Litho Ltd., Whitstable, Kent

Introduction

Eheu! fugaces, Postume, Postume,
Labunter anni . . .*
Horace. *Odes*, Book 2, 14.

As good wine needs no bush, so this book is its own best advocate. A success from the start, it has withstood the test of time, and although some forty fleeting years have slipped away since the halcyon days in which it was written, *The Magic of the Swatchways* has lost none of that fresh charm which endeared it to so many succeeding generations of young sailors and has made it the cherished possession still of countless others now no longer young.

It was when we were both very young that I first met Maurice Griffiths, and we were both equally mad about boats. He was then living in his parents' house at Ipswich, gradually building up a one-man business as a yacht broker, specialising in the older types of craft at modest prices which keen but impecunious young yachtsmen could afford to buy. I was just such a client, an undergraduate in my second year at Trinity Hall, Cambridge, and it was through his agency that I bought my first sea-going yacht, the six-ton clinker-built gaff cutter *Lily*, then laid up at Pin Mill. Thus began an enduring friendship that has continued to this day, and incidentally, Pin Mill is still my favourite home port.

*Alas! Postumus, Postumus, the flying years glide by.

In addition to running his yacht broking business, he had already begun to write articles on yachts and yachting, which found ready acceptance with the yachting press; and not long after I first met him, in 1925 he was offered the editorship of *Yacht Sales and Charters*, a new and delightful little magazine that had started to appear fortnightly, with column after column advertising yachts for sale and wanted, spiced with breezy, well-written and informative articles, generally inspired by his own genius. The success of this venture led to his appointment, with effect from January 1st, 1927, as Editor of the *Yachting Monthly* in succession to Malden Heckstall Smith. "Mr. Maurice Griffiths" ran the statement announcing this, "is a practical yachtsman, and his work as a writer on yachting matters is well known". He had still barely reached his twenty-fifth year.

A few months later, with the May issue his proud command attained its majority. "Since the *Yachting Monthly* was first launched" wrote its new Editor, reviewing twenty-one years of progress, "times have changed almost beyond belief".

Forty years on, and nearly 500 issues later, when in April, 1967, he in turn handed over to his successor, how aptly could those same words again have been applied!

A second world war, in which he served in the R.N.V.R., became a Lieutenant-Commander, and in 1940 was awarded the George Medal for courage in dismantling German magnetic mines, interrupted his editorship.

When the fighting ended and he returned to his editorial chair, gone for ever was the old world as we had known it. With the return of peace, sailing for pleasure revived and flourished on a scale hitherto unprecedented and even unimagined, but the pattern was very different.

Yet what has never changed has been the Griffiths genius, and in his long reign as Editor, he gave to the *Yachting*

Monthly a character and a quality of charm and dignity unsurpassed by any other yachting journal in the world. In a tribute published in the first issue after he had retired, the succeeding new editor, J. D. Sleightholme, wrote of his work "The Griffiths magic has been reflected in his writing, so that it has touched the lives of innumerable people. It would be hard to guess just how many of them owe the kindling of their first enthusiasm to some chance passage in *The Magic of the Swatchways*".

Echoing these words, I have always regarded it as one of the best yachting books ever written, fit to rank with Erskine Childers' *Riddle of the Sands* among the very few immortals.

It is not only as a writer, however, that countless yachtsmen are indebted to Maurice Griffiths. The Griffiths touch appeared also in his many designs for cruising yachts, of which over 800 have been built. These have nearly all been sea-kindly, simple, shoal-draft little craft, ideally suited for the shallow waters of the creeks and estuaries that their designer understood so well and loved so dearly. Not for him the long ocean passages of the globe-trotting single-hander, nor yet the hard fought contests of the ocean racer. Sailing for him has always meant the fascination of the shoals and channels of the Thames estuary, the haunting appeal of the rivers, and the lure of the little creeks stretching far inland, where peace and quiet and beauty can still be found unpolluted by the grasping hand of man.

Such peace and solitude is far more difficult to discover in the times wherein we now live than it was when *The Magic of the Swatchways* was written; but there are still places to be found where an older world of unspoiled beauty lingers on. For those who cannot experience such things directly, or who seek to live again nostalgic memories, Maurice Griffiths has captured the charm, the fascination and the calm unruffled spirit, for he, more than any other man, has been in tune with the magic that he understood so well. He has captured it for ever in the pages of this enchanting volume, for which future ages can continue to be grateful for as long as men still go sailing and the English language continues to be spoken. It must never be allowed to go out of print again.

Frank G. G. Carr.

GREENWICH
1971

Contents

PAGE

CHAPTER

I. A Chilly Introduction 17

II. Two Nights 32

III. So Little, Yet 48

IV. The Silent Creeks 65

V. The Voice of the Shingle 76

VI. Rain and Wind 93

VII. Across the Estuary 101

VIII. Rescue at Sea 120

IX. 'Wintry Weather Continuing' . . . 141

X. 'Enough to Try a Saint'. 151

XI. The Enchantment of the Sands . . . 176

XII. With *Juanita* to the 'Other Side' . . . 187

XIII. The North Sea Gale 204

XIV. Changeable Weather 221

List of Illustrations

The Magic Hour . . . . . . *Frontispiece*

Page

'Hardly a sound broke the stillness of the oncoming night' 71

'The water was creeping up to us' 103

'This was a night in a hundred'. 113

The Author 137

'*Wilful* lay . . . looking silently at her own reflection' 169

'*Juanita* had come into her own' 213

'We fought the weight of wind in that big jib' . 229

———————

Chart of the Thames Estuary . . . . 24 and 25

Foreword to the Seventh Edition

THE tides of almost forty years have ebbed and flowed into the creeks and rivers since this book was first published. During that time the yachting scene has been revolutionised and the centres where boats have their moorings are full to overflowing. To make room for the thousands of new craft being produced all the time artificial yacht harbours or marinas have been excavated from the mud flats, and where sedge grass once waved in the wind across the saltings, forests of masts now pierce the sky in orderly rows above the jetties and duckwalks of well organised yacht stations.

Where once there were hards used by the local fishermen and a few yachtsmen in their seaboots, now concrete launching pads attract hundreds of dinghies on trailers on a Saturday afternoon. In and out of the massed fleets of small craft racing speedboats buzz back and forth with water skiers weaving sloppily in their wake.

For the health of the nation as a whole it is indeed good that many times more people than ever before are able to enjoy this relaxing sport of boating in all its variety of forms. Old time yachtsmen recalling the days of quiet anchorages and scattered moorings with plenty of room to swing might be tempted to cry, Woe! All is now spoilt. But the rivers and the creeks, the outlying sands, and those shallow and often unmarked channels that lie between them—the spitways or swatchways—are as little changed as they were a century past.

With leadline and sounding pole, a little savvy and some patience the lone sailor in his little cruising boat can find quiet places here and there even now. Here he can still drop his anchor for the night away from the hum of outboard motors and the wail of transistors, and look at the sky and hear the haunting cries of the waders and gulls on the shoreline.

I know of no better contentment than this.

Maurice Griffiths.

WOODBRIDGE
SUFFOLK   1971

THE MAGIC OF THE SWATCHWAYS

I

A Chilly Introduction

A BLUSTERY north wind was blowing little scurries of snow round the corners of the deserted streets, and moaning through the telegraph wires above the local post office with a mournful wail that rose, every now and then, to an unearthly shriek. The electric-arc light that was suspended over the centre of the square where the main thoroughfare crossed the station road was swinging about in the wind, casting its cold rays up and down the fronts of the houses as it rocked, while the sign over the door of the 'Boar's Head' squealed harshly as it swung to and fro.

Two figures were making their way in the shadows down the narrow street leading to the footbridge over the railway, and as they passed, a couple of locals paused before turning into the taproom of the 'Boar's Head' and stared after them.

To explain why two somewhat determined-looking young men should be leaving behind them the cheerful lights of the little country town on this wild night and resolutely making their way towards the pitchy darkness of the river, clad in old clothes and encumbered with two suit-cases, a coil of rope, a hurricane lamp, some brown-paper parcels that cried for tender support, and a fry-pan

17

briefly clothed in a *négligée* of local news, needs but three words.

They were 'yachting.'

It was on a Saturday night in January some twelve years ago, and having just acquired sole ownership in a little 2-ton cabin-sloop called *Dabchick*, which was lying at Woodbridge in Suffolk, I had enlisted the enthusiastic help of an old school friend, Derek, who I gathered had done a little sailing in and out of this river before, to fetch the boat round to the moorings that awaited her at Ipswich.

She was but my second venture in boats—my first having been a half-share in an obstinate and altogether disastrous old 6-ton cutter which had taught me, during the previous summer, a respect for unhandy deep-keel yachts and their ways in crowded anchorages that took me years to get over.

After a season's learning aboard this heavily sparred craft drawing 5 ft. 3 in. in the Orwell River, where every mudbank had impressed itself upon my memory, I decided that the little *Dabchick* was large enough for my solitary requirements, and, after a cursory survey, had bought her with a pram-dinghy for £36. That was just after the War, when anything that had a cabin of sorts and could float of its own free will was called a yacht and fetched a high price.

To look at, *Dabchick* left a good deal to be desired if one's ideas ran on yachts glistening in the sun on the Solent. She was a converted ship's boat of uncertain age, with a transom stern, 17 ft. overall, 6 ft. beam, and drew 3 ft., with a small, lead keel bolted on the bottom of a short, false keel. Someone with a certain amount of optimism and an obvious contempt for post-war yachting parties had converted her for use as a small hireling on the Broads, and she had, in consequence, a rather neat lifting cabin-top with Willesden canvas flaps at the sides, a mast in a tabernacle, a large mainsail that was only intended for Broads sailing, plenty of lockers round the well, and a minute cabin which was my chief pride because it had two plush-cushioned berths and was fitted almost entirely in well-chosen varnished pitch-pine, while the floor was covered with real blue lino.!

That the little wretch was hard-headed, slow in stays, almost dangerously tender, narrow bowed, and, being ballasted too much by the head, was very wet and suicidal in a seaway; and that her rig of standing lug mainsail and large jib was about as mad a combination for sea sailing as could be devised, only occurred to me—by degrees—later. So also did the fact that her hull had seen better days and at least two of the planks were pulling away from their fastenings.

The man who had sold me the boat had told me he would have her ready to sail away and lying at anchor at a spot called Kison, about a mile below the town, where we should also find the dinghy on the beach. Here she would be able to lie afloat at low water and we could go aboard her as soon as we arrived by the evening train.

As we picked our way cautiously along the slippery sea-wall that the local people of Edward FitzGerald's native town refer to as The Promenade, stopping occasionally to retrieve one or other of our packages as they fell in rotation, we began to anticipate all the excitement of a 'sea passage' (as we called it) on the morrow. It was still snowing in drifts, and as we stopped

19

for a short rest under the lee of Everson's boat-building shed, the wind roared savagely through the poplars overhead, their tall heads waving violently against the gloom of the sky, while the fury of the gusts made us stagger like drunken figures.

Somehow, as the lights of the little country town were left behind and we trudged on into the nothingness that was the river, the humour of the situation, which had been buoying up my spirits since we had begun our shopping, left me, and I began to wish I hadn't been so enthusiastic about getting the boat round this week-end. That's the trouble with Derek, I was thinking; you mention a possible trip in a rash moment and he overwhelms you with his enthusiasm. The idea of going aboard a cold, cramped and obviously damp little boat on a night like this with the intention of rising early and sailing round to the Orwell became more and more repugnant as we stumbled along.

'By Jove, if we've got a breeze like this to-morrow,' Derek called boisterously over his shoulder, 'we ought to make a quick passage of it, oughtn't we?'

'Oh yes, rather, just the breeze we want,' I shouted back in the kind of voice Captain Kid might have used to encourage his crews, hoping my friend hadn't heard my teeth chatter.

At last we had reached the strip of shore at Kingston Quay and begun to search for the dinghy. My heart gave a leap as I caught sight of a dim white shape a few yards off shore and could actually hear the water washing against the bows of my new boat. Excitement and the thrill of ownership banished all misgivings I had entertained on the sea-wall.

'I say, it's a bit thick!' Derek's voice sounded plaintive

in the darkness. 'That old fool's left the dinghy too far down, and the water's covered her anchor.'

Someone had to retrieve the thing, and we tossed for it—with my usual luck. I should like to draw a veil over the next few minutes of cold misery when I slipped off my nether garments and waded in with icy water over my knees, found the dinghy's anchor by treading on one of its flukes, and then spent five minutes in the biting wind (blessing the merciful darkness, all the same) running up and down the beach to dry myself before dressing again. And when we eventually got aboard the little *Dabchick* and found the damp-smelling cabin filled with berth cushions, blankets, a sail and a heap of gear which had all been bundled on to the floor by the late owner, I would have given anything for a hot bath and a warm bed in a good hotel.

Yet an hour later we were reclining on the two berths facing one another through an atmosphere you could have cut with a knife, while the remains of a hot meal lay huddled on the locker lid which did duty as a table between us. The cabin lamp was putting up a brave fight and casting a soft, warm glow over the interior of the kennel-like cabin, while a Primus was roaring cheerfully on the floor, heating up a saucepan full of good coffee.

As I lay back on my berth and gazed with glassy eyes through rings of tobacco smoke at the cabin-top beams, I would not have changed places with any other mortal in the world. It would have called for too much effort, for one thing. The little boat, sheering about in the squalls and snubbing occasionally on her anchor chain, was quivering with life and warmth and companionship, the wind was moaning through her rigging (the expression attracted me at the moment) and the little waves were breaking along her clinker-built sides with sudden rushes of sound. The possession of one's first boat and all its attendant interests and novelties is an experience which is to be remembered for the rest of one's life.

And later that night, as we lay in our berths under warm blankets, sleep withheld her spell for a time while we listened to all the unaccustomed noises, trying to diagnose each one. The sudden rasp of the anchor chain on the bobstay, the *tap, tap,* of a halliard on the mast, the occasional squeak of a block in its eye-bolt, the *scrunch* of the water against the lands of the planks, and over all the continuous roar of the wind in the trees that sheltered this snug anchorage.

Once, as we dozed off, the cry of a curlew, faint and shrill, came from far down the river. It sounded plaintive out there in the cold, windy night, while in here it was so warm . . .

I awoke with that peculiar stiff and uncomfortable feeling that one gets from sleeping in an unheated boat in winter. The temperature in the cabin had undergone a change during the night. In fact, it was now so nearly arctic that staying in one's bunk with the hope of getting warm again was out of the question. We had left the cabin-top raised to give us air, and the draught that was pouring in through the gap above the door penetrated the blankets like a knife.

I shut up the air inlet and lit the Primus, but it was not until the coffee was put by to keep warm and the bacon was sizzling in the pan that my companion fully opened the eye that had been fluttering for some time and made a poor pretence at waking up with a start of surprise.

'Good Heavens, I haven't overslept, have I?'

I said, Oh no, he surely knew that I was by nature an early riser? Apparently he did not.

'But—it's hardly light yet.'

I glanced out at the grey sky that was only just beginning to pale in the east.

'No, it's only seven o'clock; you needn't get up yet. I thought you'd like breakfast in bed.'

He sank back with a sigh of relief.

'By Jove, Maurice,' he said magnanimously. 'Your brain must be as good as new.'

If we had hoped for considerably less wind (although neither of us had dared express the wish) we were disappointed, for it was blowing as hard as ever when we started to get under way about nine o'clock, and the squalls were coming out of a grey, snow-laden sky. The wind had backed more to the west, but it was every bit as piercing.

'Now for a fine s-sail!' Derek cried as he started to tie in reef-points, but the remark, begun well, ended on a slightly *tremolo* note that rather spoilt the effect. I dared not risk my voice and remained silent.

We tied in the second reef, for we found that the big lugsail, intended for the Broads, had only two reefs. There still seemed a great deal of it when it was set, slamming about in the gusts. There was, we found, only one jib, and that was big enough to fill the whole fore triangle when set on a 5-ft. bowsprit.

'Never mind, she'll carry it!'

Derek's enthusiasm was infectious, and when he broke out the anchor, *Dabchick* started off down the narrow channel like a rocket. The little boat almost took charge, and it was all I could do with both hands wrenching at the short tiller to keep off the bank.

The Thames Estuary

Only the more important sands and shoals, buoys, beacons, light-houses and light-vessels are shown here. But there are many, many more to puzzle the mariner in this corner of the North Sea.

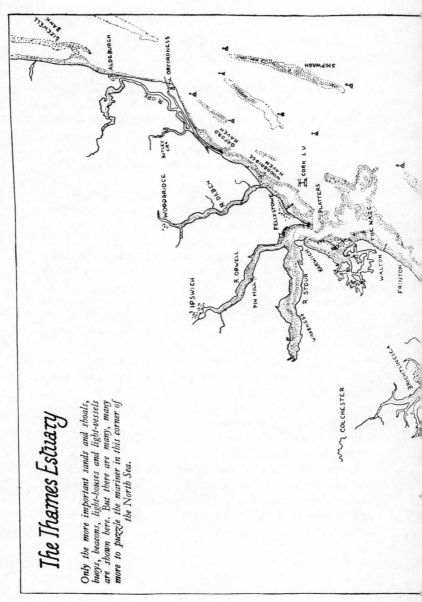

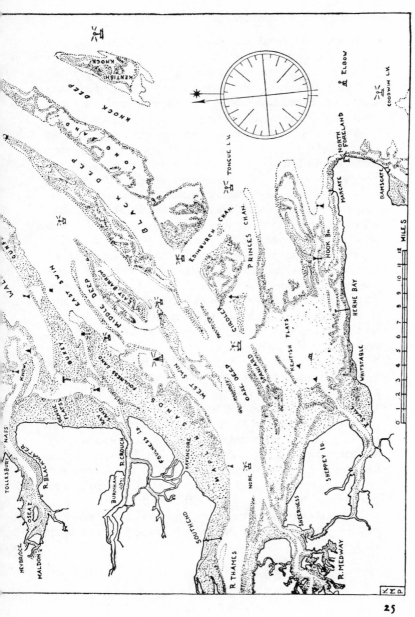

At the first bend we had to gybe. Derek began to haul in the mainsheet.

'Keep her going until I get this swigged right in,' he said breathlessly, and as he did so the boom flew over with a crash and laid *Dabchick* on her side until the water poured over the well coamings, then she righted herself.

We were so surprised to find the boat upright and the mast still standing that we shook hands over our good fortune. And while my attention was thus taken up, *Dabchick* took a wild sheer and nearly mounted the bank. However, the interval gave us time to breathe, and the flood-tide, aided with the boathook, floated us off in a quarter of an hour, and we continued our somewhat erratic progress down the river.

Off Waldringfield the channel widened, and even on this cold, blustering day the Deben looked pretty in the pale light of an obscured sun. The bare trees were waving their branches at us as the squalls tore through them, stripping them of twigs, while their nakedness was enhanced by the white patches of snow that lay here and there in the fields.

As we rounded into Ramsholt Reach we brought the wind forward of our starboard beam, and with her sails sheeted in, *Dabchick* lay over in the squalls until the water lapped into the well. At times she was overpowered, and we had to ease the jib sheet to let her luff up a little into the wind. This jib of hers was too big for the reefed mainsail and was holding her head down, causing her to carry lee helm. It had no reef-points, and neither of us knew enough then to take in a temporary reef with stopping at the head.

It was about high water now, and by the time we were passing the collection of forlorn-looking motor-boats and fishing craft moored above Felixstowe Ferry the ebb had begun to race out through the narrows between the shingle banks.

The sight that met our inexperienced eyes as we turned the last corner and opened up the bar made our hearts miss a beat. The entrance appeared to be an unbroken mass of white foam with leaping crests, whose tops tumbled over and were carried along like steam by the wind. For one moment it was on the tip of my tongue to suggest running back, but there was a six-knot ebb carrying us ruthlessly towards that barrier of shoals and broken water, and, sailing her hardest, *Dabchick* would not have been able to forge against it.

There was no turning back now.

As he had professed a slight knowledge of the lie of the channel over this bar, Derek took the helm while I held on to the weather coaming and watched the banks of shingle on either side racing past. A coastguardsman came running down to the point from the Martello tower, and as we drew abreast he asked our name and where we were bound.

'*Dabchick*, bound for Ipswich!' I yelled with pride.

'You'll soon be back,' was all he shouted as we swept past.

A minute later we buried our bowsprit into the first of the breakers, a sea leapt up, filled our jib and the sail burst with a noise like a gunshot. At the same instant our keel hit the shingle with a jarring crash that pitched us both to the lee side of the well.

Dabchick lifted her foredeck clear of the welter of water, rose on a comber, staggered on and crashed once more on the hard shingle. A third time she lifted and fell, while a sea broke on to her weather deck and

27

poured into the well, and then she lay on her beam ends while the furious tide swirled around her, pressing her harder on to the dreaded bank and bringing the pram dinghy alongside to leeward.

'My God!' cried Derek, as he scrambled up to the windward side. 'I've piled you on.'

The remnants of the jib were flogging away to leeward in long streamers, the violence of their antics shaking the masthead. All around us was a seething welter of foam and water, while the roaring of the seas on the bar and the continual thuds as they broke against our weather side filled our ears with a terrifying tumult of sound.

My attention was arrested by my companion, who was hurriedly slipping off various garments without a thought to his innate modesty or the perishing cold. The horrible thought occurred to me that the strain had been too much for him—Derek, I had always thought, possessed a delicately balanced mind, and now in this emergency——

'I've put you on, old man,' he explained, looking rather like a ballet girl as he fluttered, so to speak, in the wind, 'and I'm jolly well going to get you off. So here g-goes!'

And before I could protest he had slipped overboard up to his waist. The boat moved as soon as he jumped from her, and when he put his shoulder under her quarter she gave one more scrunch and sailed off, dragging him with her.

'I'm all right!' he cried, as I tried to haul him aboard, 'keep her going till we're over the bar.'

The next few minutes were a nightmare, for the little boat was quite unable to cope with the steep, curling seas and simply dived into the heart of them, burying her foredeck to the mast and wallowing under the weight of water. Every moment I expected to feel her hit the ground again, but mercifully she was swept clear into deeper water, where the seas were more regular, and I was able to round her up into the wind and help my friend aboard.

'Near thing. All my fault; I hugged the shore too close,' was all he said as he disappeared into the cabin to dry himself. My thanks seemed absurdly inadequate in the circumstances.

When he came out into the well again, fully dressed, and took the helm, I clambered forward to take in what remained of our jib. It looked too much like a signal of distress to be left up.

Sitting astride the mast tabernacle, I hauled in the flogging strips of canvas while the lean-headed little boat dived into half a dozen successive seas, drenching me and sending a lot of water below, squirting through a dozen places in the forehatch and cabin-top.

For four hours we tried to beat against the strong ebb that was pouring north against us, while the squalls laid us almost flat and the salt spray and sleet blinded us. The boat, with no headsail and a mainsail that was obviously too large, reefed as it was, proved almost unmanageable, carrying prodigious weather helm and getting into irons every time we went about. Had I known then how to counteract this, I should willingly have hove-to and moved half the ballast further aft. As it was we thrashed on, grimly fighting every inch of the way and anxiously watching our pathetically slow progress each time we stood in on the port tack towards Felixstowe.

That was the coldest and most miserable passage I

29

have ever made. We were able to stand only short spells at the helm, and I well remember the agony of aching hands as one sat in the bucking cabin, trying to get back one's circulation in the brief spell below, while the increasing bilge water surged up on to the lee berth.

By the time we had brought Languard Point at the entrance of Harwich Harbour in sight through a break in a sleet squall, the ebb-tide had eased, and another board allowed us to fetch through the shallow swatch-way that used to lie in those days between the end of the jetty and the deadly Platter Sands.

Here an unexpected cross sea suddenly rose above us to windward, tumbled over and fell with a thunderous crash on our deck, seething over the cabin-top and surging into the well. For one sickening moment, as the water boiled around our feet and burst open the cabin doors, it seemed that the little boat had filled and was going down under us; but she slowly shook herself free of the water, lurched on and rounded the point into the harbour, very much down by the head with the weight of water inside her.

While we raced up the smooth water of the harbour I bailed with a bucket until the bilge water was below the floorboards once more; then I lit the Primus and handed out a mug of steaming Bovril to the mate who had so unselfishly risked his life for the sake of my boat.

An hour later, when we lay snugly on my moorings at Ipswich, with the gear stowed and a hot meal under way, we sat in the cramped little cabin, drying ourselves, and declared that, now it was over, it had been a great passage and the boat herself a 'wonderful sea-boat' to have stood it. And the joy of ownership that I felt then, the mounting enthusiasm that swept over me like a flood, glossed over all its trials and hardships, its dangers and miseries, and I wanted to do it again, to go and explore other rivers and estuaries in her—for she was mine. My boat!

The joy of that moment lingers still.

II

Two Nights

HOOK'S aweigh. You might break out the fores'l.'
As I stood on the foredeck and hauled in the
last few fathoms of dripping cable, the mate
broke out the tanned roller foresail and *Wild Lone*
slowly gathered way before the light westerly air. With
the anchor catted and the chain all stowed below, I
paused for a minute on the foredeck and gazed aft.

Already Paglesham Hard with the big shed overlooking
it was fading in the gloom astern, and naught but a
faint reddish glow over the fields and trees beyond
Rochford now remained of the wonderful sunset which,
but a quarter of an hour before, had filled the whole of
the sky in the west and cast beams of flaming light
on the rolling nebulae that had hovered over the eastern
horizon like vast mountains of burnished gold. The
sidelights were casting their distinctive gleams alternately on the foresail as it bellied first one side and then
the other. The light of the cabin lamp, turned low,
filtered through the three round deadlights in each
side-coaming, and played in three yellow patches on the
varnished rail.

Compared with the little *Dabchick*, this 5-ton sloop
seemed to possess a fine expanse of deck, and I walked
aft without holding on to anything, just to prove it.
I was *proud* to possess a boat like this. With a spoon

32

bow and a transom stern *Wild Lone* was not unlike a
big dinghy in shape, having a perfectly flat floor amidships, with rounded bilges. Twenty-four feet overall,
22 ft. on the waterline and with just over 8 ft. beam,
she drew but 21 in. with the centreboard and iron
rudder plate hauled up. There was a cabin eight feet
long, which seemed palatial after *Dabchick's* little kennel,
and, in addition, there was a fo'c'sle which had a
folding-cot berth, so that three could sleep aboard.
The centreboard case divided the cabin floor in two,
but it allowed a very large flap-table to be fitted, on
which a full-size chart could be spread out.

After one season with *Dabchick*, in which I had explored
alone all the creeks and anchorages between the Woodbridge River and Burnham-on-Crouch, I found I wanted
a bigger boat with not such cramped accommodation,
and one particularly which would not lie at a crazy
angle when she took the mud on the ebb. *Dabchick*
had taught me a great deal about handling a boat, for
it had been a stormy season and I had sailed mostly
alone by choice. My little boat had supplied all the
companionship I had needed. I had made my first
single-handed coastal passage in her; I had experienced
the eternal wonder of my first night-passage alone; I
had almost lost her in an unexpected gale that put her
on a lee shore one night and threatened to break her
up before I could haul her off; I had learned what fear
was on another occasion when caught out in a bad
squall when a lump of displaced ballast started a plank
and I had to bail frantically as she ran back to Harwich
with the bilge water up to the level of her berths . . .
I had grown fond of her, because she and I had come
through so much together, that windy summer, but I

knew she was not 'man enough' and actually not sound
enough for coastal exploration.

Therefore I sold her and bought this 5-tonner, which
I renamed *Wild Lone*, for with her, like the cat in Kipling
that 'walked by himself,' I wanted to go by my wild
lone to the wild, wet waters; 'for all places were alike
to me.' But I was not always single-handed, and on this
particular night I had a cheerful mate who had joined
the ship for a week's cruise to the Crouch and Roach
Rivers.

There was by now very little of the wind that had
blown so fresh all day long, and as the trim little sloop
glided with the ebb past the fast uncovering mudbanks,
down the narrow Roach and so into the Crouch, her
forefoot turned over the water with a gentle, undulating
trickle like the sound of a mountain stream chuckling
past clean-swept pebbles. It was to be a night in a hundred
—calm, intense, mysterious—the kind of night when
one's only wish is to sail away to some unheard-of
island and never to return to the incessant struggle for
life in big cities.

Otherwise silent and motionless at the helm, the mate
was softly whistling a haunting waltz, and somehow
it seemed that a curlew, whose shrill cry rose above the
sedge grass over towards Havengore, had also become
magnetized by the refrain, for his tiny voice called
in unison. I sat down in a corner of the well and
propped my head against the cabin bulkhead. The
waltz came to a close, and the mate's teeth sparkled
in the narrow beam of light that escaped past the cabin
doors.

'Good job we've got this ebb,' he murmured, 'the
wind will soon die right away, I'm thinking.'

I nodded sleepily and did not reply. His voice sounded very far away.

'. . . and as there hasn't been a breath for the last half-hour, I think I might leave the helm with safety and warm that coffee up.'

I stirred lazily and discovered that it had gone colder and that I felt stiff and uncomfortable. The mate left the helm and peered at me.

'Oh, so you're awake at last?'

I remarked that any idiot could see that I hadn't been asleep, considering I had only sat there for five minutes.

'Five minutes, eh? Do you know we left the Crouch with the last of that breeze nearly an hour ago and have been drifting on the ebb ever since? Do you know where you are?'

I raised myself on one elbow and looked over the coaming. We were at sea. The land whence we had come was invisible but for one solitary yellow light that was probably the riding light of a smack anchored in the mouth of the Crouch. It all seemed unreal and strange, this sudden transition from the Roach below Paglesham to the loneliness of the sea. I began to feel that I really must have gone to sleep, especially as I began to feel as though I had been sitting on a knobbly, hard seat for about ten hours.

Not a breath stirred. The little ship scarcely moved, but as she rolled almost imperceptibly on the steady swell her boom rose and fell wearily, and the drooping mainsheet tried again and again to raise itself clear of the still water. Far away off our starboard beam, over the rim of the world in which we floated, the tip of a ball of copper was appearing, suffusing the heavens around it with a faint, reddish glow like the night reflection of a city seen far away. Even as I looked, little by little it increased in size, and tentatively its golden trail felt its way across the unbroken mirror-like surface of the water towards us. And as though basking in the oncoming splendour of the harvest moon, the bosom of the sea heaved gently, as though it slept peacefully.

On such a night as this the whole world seems to doze, and time itself pauses in its headlong career. Above, in the velvety vastness of the heavens, countless stars twinkled and coquetted with one another, whilst their counterparts rocked and reeled with silent laughter from the surface of the water. Far away off the starboard bow a fainter and paler glare in the sky seemed to mimic the delicate radiance of the rising moon. That was Clacton, and it seemed incongruous to think that the pier and promenade would now be a scene of gaiety, light and laughter, whilst out here scarcely a thing moved and silence reigned unbroken.

A sudden flash of white light glared in my eyes for a few seconds and was gone. Peering closely in its direction, I could just make out the crisp silhouette of a gas buoy. Its white occulting light flashed out again, reaching towards us along the surface of the water with a twisting, broken finger. Again it was gone. As I watched it, and counted the seconds while its brilliant light flashed on and off, it gradually approached the track of the moon. For five seconds it hovered in line with the semi-circle of copper beyond the far horizon, every part of its iron cage, every bar and rod and piece of ironwork clearly defined, then it was the other side and drifting away again. I recognized it as the West Buxey, and was glad, for it meant that the ebb was carrying us truly down the Raysand Channel.

36

'Looks like a faint breeze coming up from the east'ard.'

The mate's voice behind me brought me out of my reverie, and I found him offering me a steaming cup of coffee. Half-way along the moon track the oily water was marked by a line of ripples that gradually approached. Later the first puff reached us, a faint breath that kissed the cheek and brushed affectionately against the dark surface of the mainsail, so that the reef points ceased to patter and the mainsheet rose reluctantly from the water. Then it was gone again and the surface of the water remained untroubled. But soon the first of the ripples, flashing in the starlight, were around us, and the little ship began to feel the light air that pressed the folds out of her sails, and as she began to awaken to life once more the dinghy hurried after her, chuckling with glee at this new effort on the part of its mistress.

The rhythmetic glare of the West Buxey buoy was now far astern, and no longer was the buoy itself visible : but before long another shape slowly loomed into view off the starboard bow—gaunt, angular, and lifeless, like the signpost at the four cross-roads, incongruous out here at sea, yet an old friend—the Buxey beacon. And as it hovered weirdly on our beam the friendly little breeze died away as quietly as it had come, and we were again left to drift silently on the north-running ebb. The moon had now risen from the edge of the sea, and as the hours passed she rose majestically into the depths of the sky, whilst her trail, now silver, flashed and sparkled with phosphorescent light.

So we continued to drift, and the light of the Knoll buoy flashed closer and closer off our starboard bow. I looked up at the lifeless burgee and sighed contentedly.

'This won't get us into Mersea. We're being carried

37

towards the Wallet, and there won't be any wind till morning. Better let go here and go in on the morning's flood.'

While the anchor sank fathoms deep to the sandy bottom beneath, and the chain rattled noisily after it, the mate lowered the mainsail and buried himself with the tiers.

'No use bothering about the riding light,' he said, looking astern, 'it's getting lighter in the east already.'

The night was over, for the approaching dawn began to play in pale streaks of light on the little yacht's white transom as she rode patiently to her anchor in the utter solitude and silence of the sea.

.   .   .   .   .

There was another night whose details will always remain in my memory. In a burst of enthusiasm, my friend D. and I left Harwich just before sunset with the intention of sailing *Albatross* round to West Mersea, where she was to be laid up, for that uncertain summer of '22 had passed, autumn was upon us, and all self-respecting yachts by this time were finding mudberths for the winter.

The distance that D., who lived far inland, had to travel to reach the boat necessitated our making the passage this week-end, unless the weather proved absolutely impossible. It looked as though it might, as we plunged out past the Beach End bell-buoy and headed into a short sea that was rolling up from the Naze, for the sun was sinking into a barrier of ugly-looking black clouds with yellow-tipped edges as sharp as a saw-blade.

It was altogether a mad time to start on a long beat

against a fresh south-westerly wind up the Wallet, for we had about four hours of ebb yet to run against us, which would make progress, once round the Naze, deadly tedious. But we had started because D., having arrived by train two hours before, could not rest until we got under way—'for anywhere, old man. But let's get under way, and we might as well make it Mersea!'

It was useless to point out that the tide was wrong, the wind was obviously going to blow hard after sundown, and it would be far better to wait a few hours and take the whole of the flood with us. D. is of that dangerous type of shipmate—entirely likeable, irrepressibly enthusiastic and casual to a criminal degree about seamanlike essentials. His excess of high spirits carries you beyond your reason, and the usual preparations against emergencies which every seaman learns to make are ignored.

Night had definitely closed in by the time we had the Naze Point abeam and slowly opened out the lights of Walton. There was a high, lumpy sea running, and already *Albatross*, with one reef in her mainsail, was driving her lean bows into the heart of every other wave. It was already pitch dark, and this made it quite impossible to watch the seas as they raced towards us and luff up accordingly. Only the flash of a breaking crest gave one any warning of the crash and the cloud of driving spray that would follow.

Albatross was not making good weather of it. She was a tender little craft with a bad-shaped, low spoon-bow and scarcely any sheer, an old Nore One Design, of which several had been built for racing off Southend. With a sloop rig of racing area, she measured 22 ft. by 7 ft. beam, and drew just under 3 ft. with the iron centreboard

39

up, and I recall her as the wettest and most comfortless boat I have ever had. Yet at first I had been attracted by her speed and general handiness.

We were making very slow progress against the ebb tide, and the lights of Frinton seemed to keep their position for a depressing length of time. Suddenly a more violent squall burst upon us, with rain, and *Albatross* lay over until the jet-black water poured into her large well and a sea broke clean over her foredeck.

D. at once began to scramble forward, shouting directions which were carried away by the wind, so that I got only snatches of them:

'. . . Another reef . . . keep her sailing . . . ease her . . . claw-ring . . .'

While he worked the peak halliard and the ratchet reefing-gear handle at the mast, I stood up and tried to assist the straining canvas to roll neatly into the claw-ring on the boom, but a sudden dive on the part of the boat all but threw me out of the well, and when I picked myself up off the lee-coaming there was a rent a foot long in the sail. My voice sounded inadequate as I shouted to the dark figure bunched up against the mast, but he heard, and in a few minutes we had three reefs rolled in the mainsail and the tear covered up.

Albatross was easier now, but nothing could stop her from pounding as her U-shaped bow dropped into the inky hollows, and it seemed inconceivable that her lightly-built hull could put up with the terrific slamming and jarring and not open all its seams.

'Better keep over to the Gunfleet side,' D. shouted once; 'we might get a bit of a lee off the sands.'

The lights of Clacton, appearing every now and then as we lifted over a rushing crest, were far away yet, for we were a long way from the coast. Presently D., who had been sitting huddled up in the lee of the cabin-top, leaned over the lee-coaming, and with a feeling of compassion I realized his unhappiness. He was not ill for long, however, and began his trick at the helm soon after, while I sat on the floor of the well, watching the dim shapes of the seas as they raced away from our lee quarter into the darkness.

Instead of getting a lee under the sands, we found the wind blowing straight down the Wallet and the seas becoming more and more dangerous for a boat like this. Her foredeck was being constantly swept, and there was a good deal of water coming over into the well, while heavy lumps of spray were occasionally thudding into the mainsail, threatening to burst it. . . .

Presently D. leaned down and said something to me I could not hear. I stood up, receiving a dash of spray on my chest that nearly winded me, and he repeated his question. It sounded like Chinese, and as I noticed the haggard, drawn look that had suddenly come into his face (he was twice my own age) the horror of what the effect the night might have had on his mind struck me. Again he bawled something, pointing forward, and I thought I caught the words 'open portlight,' or something like them.

Then I realized what he was trying to say, but why he didn't say it I could not make out, but did not stop to find out. Diving into the dimly-lit cabin, I confirmed my fears. The seas, dashing against the forward cabin-coaming, had smashed the glass of the large rectangular portlight, and even as I crouched there a flood of water poured into the cabin and over our blankets, which were strapped on the top of the centreboard case. I took a

41

sodden cushion and rammed it into the aperture, stopping the immediate cascade.

Hurled against the lee-side of the cabin by the wild motion, I found the bilge water over my ankles, and discovered that the lee-berth was awash. For a moment my heart almost stopped as I realized how much water the boat must be making.

I crawled into the cramped fo'c'sle, where the pounding sounded like thunder, and struck a match. The seams were working and water was trickling in here and there, and I hoped, as the match went out, that the broken portlight was responsible for most of the bilge water. It was a pity, however, that the only way we hoped to keep our blankets dry aboard this pitiful boat, by strapping them in a bundle over the table, had proved useless. All the bedding was by now soaked with salt water.

It was at this moment, when I was crawling feet first out of the fo'c'sle, that the boat gave a sudden lurch and a metallic crash jarred her from keel to truck. The shock threw me against the centreboard case, half stunning me for the moment, while the boat rose to a crest and dropped again to crash once more.

'My God, we're on the sands!'

D.'s alarmed shout brought me to my senses, and I hauled desperately at the centreboard tackle which was made fast at the after end of the case.

For a minute, perhaps, with the centreboard up, *Albatross* sailed on, and D. tried to get her round on to the port tack. But a breaking sea drove her head off again, and a moment later she struck once more, this time with her keel.

'Ease off the mainsheet! We'll try to gybe her off!'

It was a desperate remedy, but I saw my shipmate's

42

idea and let the mainsheet run. She swung round until her quarter faced the seas, then she stopped. Each time a sea lifted her she only moved farther on to the sands with a sickening thud.

'It's no go,' I shouted, chagrined at the failure of a desperate plan that, nevertheless, frequently gets a boat off, 'we must get the canvas off her.'

Stowing the sails as the boat rolled and shuddered, while occasional seas broke with a thud against her quarter and drove in sheets into the well, was a difficult task. When it was done, I got the anchor ready. *Albatross* could not be left in this position with her stern to the wind. It was no good just dropping the anchor here; she would have sat on it and holed herself. The hook would have to be carried out in the dinghy.

'Dinghy?' D. said in dismay. 'It's gone!'

And he held up the straggled end of the broken painter.

The dinghy had disappeared into the night, when, Heaven alone knew; *Albatross* was lying in a dangerous position with her quarter to wind and seas, slowly bumping farther on to the sands, and the anchor had to be let go to windward to bring her head round without a moment's delay, for the tide was dropping fast.

Sounding with a boathook, I found about 3 ft. round us, and the bottom as hard as a gravel path. There was nothing for it. Soaked as I was already, I waved aside D.'s rash but sporting offer to go, jumped in and carried the anchor about 30 ft. to windward. Then we hauled in on the cable and were thankful to find the boat slowly turn round until she lay broadside on to the wind. She would move no farther, and we had to leave her like that, heeled over to port and being pounded by the seas against her weather bilge.

43

Gradually, however, the waves abated as the tide dropped, and in an hour *Albatross* was high and dry on the Gunfleet Sands, about four miles off Clacton. We bailed all the water out of the boat with a bucket, praying that her hull was not badly damaged. Then, in the comfortless inclined cabin the shipmate managed to light the Primus, which helped to warm us and soon gave us steaming mugs of Oxo.

It was while our spirits were thus being revived that I suddenly remembered how drawn my friend's usually cheery face had looked earlier in the night, and how he hadn't been able to speak properly. He was certainly his old self again now, but it wasn't until I mentioned as tactfully as possible the fright he had given me that I learned the reason. The poor man, to prevent personal loss, had bravely, so to speak, been sailing with the helm in one hand and his teeth in the other!

Our position was a desperate one. If there was the same amount of sea running when the tide turned and came round us, there would be every chance of the boat breaking up under us before she could float off. If the ship went to pieces there was no dinghy to take to, and the sands were isolated and would be completely covered at high water.

The red flash of the Gunfleet lighthouse, standing on piles on the outer edge of the sands some four miles away, was clearly visible, and a flare would probably have attracted attention, or even brought the Clacton lifeboat out. But there was nothing dry enough at present to burn aboard for a flare, and after discussing the matter, we decided to stand by the ship and do our best to save her.

It seemed very lonely and forlorn out there; the wind

44

moaned continually through the rigging, its note rising and falling, the halliards rattled furiously on the mast, occasional rain squalls pattered on the sloping weather topsides, and over all there was a sound that one seemed to sense rather than hear, an ominous, deep roaring, like the noise of an angry mob—the seas breaking on the sands a hundred yards away.

Once we went out for a run across the sands to help our circulation, splashing through the innumerable puddles trapped in the ridges left by the waves; then we carried the anchor farther out towards the deep water and sank it well into the sand, for on its ability to hold our lives possibly depended. After that we returned to the damp, stuffy cabin, and sat close to the roaring Primus, trying to suppress our anxiety while the tide turned.

That waiting was the worst part of it all, and those hours of darkness seemed interminable. The alarum clock said half-past four when the water first began to gurgle round our keel. We should either be afloat or a mass of drifting matchwood before daylight came. The wind had not abated, and although the rain had ceased there was a keenness in the air that seemed to cut through one's damp clothes.

Slowly the water covered the sand in our vicinity, and the waves, small and playful as yet, slapped our weather bilge and shook the boat. Then, as they broke more heavily against her, she began to lift and fall gently. Her keel was grinding in the sand, and her mast was rising and falling, and rising a little higher with each scend of the sea.

The waves became heavier, more insistent, and broke with a crash against her, shaking her little, white hull

45

and lifting her, only to be dropped again on to the cruel sand, while her gear rattled and her hull groaned under the shocks. Anxiously we crawled below and examined the timbers by the light of a candle, for we expected to find them broken and her seams letting in a flood of water, but as yet she was standing up to the pounding.

Soon she was upright and thudding on the sand only with her iron keel. Each time a sea broke against her and dashed in spray over the cabin-top and into the well, she lifted, hovered on the crest for a moment, slewed her stern round a little more to leeward, then dropped with a jarring crash. Again and again. Surely the hull could not stand much more of this! Yet she was not making any water.

At last she was head to wind, lifting gamely over the steep seas to thud on the sand while the anchor chain snubbed with fearful bangs, threatening to pull out the samson post, or part one of its links.

'Thank Heaven we dug that hook in!' D. called out once. 'If that didn't hold, nothing could save us. Come on, let's get the mains'l up.'

She was almost afloat now, hitting the bottom at longer intervals. When the mainsail was set, I went forward to try to haul in the cable. As I caught hold of it, a bigger comber than usual came rushing down on us, its crest glistening in the first light of the coming dawn. *Albatross* lifted her bow as it broke over her foredeck, while I made a frantic grab at the mast; the cable snubbed with a heavy bang, and the boat dropped into the hollow to crash once more on the sand.

As she rose to the next sea, I grasped the cable and hauled it in. There was no strain on it.

'My God, the cable's parted!'

46

Almost before I cried out, *Albatross* had been carried to leeward, and once more she slewed round and lay pounding on the sands. My heart sank, as it seemed for a moment as though we were doomed now; but, as fortune would have it, when she struck, the little boat had turned round to starboard, and she now lay with her bowsprit pointing towards Clacton lights—and the deeper water of the Wallet. If she would only sail off . . .

'Loose the foresail!'

With her mainsheet pinned in and the foresail drawing, *Albatross* lay over on her side, pounding badly on her lee-bilge. But as she rose to each sea she forged ahead a few feet, dropped, banged on the sand, rose, sailed ahead again, dropped, sailed a little longer, pounded a little less violently, and at last hit the sand no more.

She was sailing again.

In the east the false dawn had paled the sky, grey, cold and cheerless. Yet it was a grand sight to our weary, salt-encrusted eyes, and as we thrashed the little boat up past the flashing Knoll buoy, past the North-West Knoll and the spherical Bench Head buoy, driving our bows into the short seas of the Blackwater on our last boards into Mersea Quarters, we blessed the coming of the day, for it meant that what was, we hoped, the worst night of our lives, was over.

III

So Little, Yet . . .

WITH the perspiration running down my face, I dropped my suit-case and oilskin on the grass bank and sat down with a sigh. Each time the dusty road from Maldon East Station to Heybridge Lock seems to grow longer, and, arrayed as I was in sea-boots and the extra clothes squeezed out of an already overcrowded case, I found the afternoon sun exhausting.

From where I lay on the cool grass in front of the yacht club house the familiar scene gave a sense of repose after the rush of trains and buses. The ebb had been silently receding for nearly three hours, and on each side of the river the mudflats were uncovering rapidly. A small white-sailed barge-yacht was trying to beat up against a dying westerly wind, and on the horizon, it seemed, Osea lay like a mirage with its purple undulating masses of trees. My eyes wandered listlessly over the few yachts riding to their moorings in Collier's Reach, and came to rest on the trim 7-ton yawl which was to be my home for the next three days.

Far away across the fields the chimes of Maldon church rang out sonorously. Five o'clock. I rested my head in the palms of my hands and stared lazily up at the deep-blue sky. It seemed so peaceful.

Footsteps scrunching along the gravel path just above my head brought me to earth again. They stopped
48

hesitatingly, and I turned to meet the cheery face of the man who looked after my friend's yacht.

'Good afternoon, sir. Mr. Mortimore hasn't arrived yet, although he said he'd be here by fower.' His eyes turned to the yacht as she lay tugging gently at her mooring chain. He stood thus for several seconds, in his old eyes that far-away, dreamy look that comes to those who live all their lives on or near the sea. Then he added: 'There won't be much water under her now, I reckon, and if you want to start to-night you'd better take her down to the first buoy opposite Northey. She'll lie afloat there, sir, and you can pick your friend up from Mill Beach, just opposite there. I'll help you if you like, of course.'

Thanking him for his advice, I declined the old man's offer, as I knew that a tea-table awaited him in the little cottage near the post office. So, picking up my belongings and trying to force myself to realize that 'Time and tide wait for no man,' I walked down to the dinghy, and was thankful for the first time that day that I was wearing my knee-boots. Not all the mud at Heybridge is hard enough to walk on. There was obviously no time to be lost if I wanted to keep the boat afloat, and with unusual energy I dragged the reluctant staysail out of the overcrowded sail locker. I knew that the motor was in running order, but in such ideal surroundings the throb and clatter of an old engine would seem almost a sacrilege.

The blocks creaked as I hoisted the mizen, and as if in answer to that stirring sound came the shrill call of a curlew from somewhere on the little sedge-covered island that is called Northey. Then others took up the song, and I found my pulse beating with suppressed

49

excitement as I threw the mooring buoy overboard. It seemed as if that simple action had severed my connexion with the life on shore; that I had thereby cut adrift the ties of convention, the unrealities and illusions of cities and crowds; that I was free now, free to go where I chose, to do and to live and to conquer as I liked, to play the game wherein a man's qualities count for more than his appearance.

Far off down the river came that call again. Shrill, abrupt, penetrating, it demanded an answer. And, as if she heard, the old ship seemed to strain forward on the sluicing ebb; the blue water parted at her stem and turned over into two diverging lines of chuckling ripples.

The black buoy was steadily drawing closer. With the tide sluicing part its rusty sides, it rolled and swayed drunkenly, turning round first to the left, pausing, then to the right, bowing grotesquely first to the Northey shore, then to the Mill Beach shore, green weed hanging from its water-mark and swaying in the fast-running water.

For a moment it hovered abeam; then it had dropped astern and the old vessel forged ahead, eager to be at sea once again.

'*Bint*, aho-ooo-oy!'

The familiar voice, thundering across the receding water, startled me. Of course, the owner had arrived. Down went the helm; reluctantly, as though she hated delay of this sort, the yacht swung round head to wind and tide, her sails shaking restlessly, and over went the anchor with a rattle of chain.

Half an hour later the dinghy grounded opposite the club house once more and, panting, I shipped the oars

after a tough pull against the fast-running ebb. My
friend extended a brown hand.

'You're a nice chap,' he laughed, showing two rows
of white, even teeth, 'pinching a fellow's ship and
running away with her. If I hadn't called you, you'd
have been dreaming past Osea by now!'

Humble explanations that it was neither felonious
intention nor mental aberration on my part, but solely
a question of the depth of water off Heybridge club
house at low tide that had prompted me to take his
ship down the river, appeased my friend's wrath. Then,
chatting in subdued voices, we floated down on the latter
half of the ebb while the saltings on Northey slipped
silently by.

We were alongside the yacht almost before we realized
it, so strong is the tide here. How trim she looked!
How dainty lying there, her new burgee flapping at the
head of a newly varnished mast, her glistening topsides
reflected faithfully on the almost glassy surface of the
water, the delicate tracery of her rigging standing out
so clearly against the deep blue of the sky. Yet, how
strong she was, with those powerful bows that have
smashed many a green wave into scintillating foam
when those smooth sides have been groaning under the
terrific onslaught of a hard sou'-wester in the Wallet.

She curtsied slowly to us as we stepped on to her
deck, as though to welcome her owner. She knew. And
the halliards ceased momentarily to quiver in the gentle
breeze as if to pay homage to their master; and far away
again came that shrill call of a curlew, his tiny form
hidden by the high grass on Northey Island.

'What shall we have for tea?'

My friend's matter-of-fact voice broke upon my musing

51

with startling suddenness. Hadn't he seen how his ship had welcomed him? Hadn't he heard that call? Weren't his veins tingling with excitement, his pulse beating at the romance that lay beyond those wooded hills, where the sea even now was tumbling and sparkling in the waning sunlight? I fear that my reply, as a guest, was unnecessarily abrupt.

'Oh, anything.'

Lying at full length on the after-deck, I looked far down into the green depths and counted the jelly-fish as their transparent, delicate forms floated languidly by. Invertebrate life, devoid of intelligence and feeling; was Man thus, far back through countless ages? And had he, through numberless reincarnations, experienced those lessons that have imperceptibly improved and improved him, until, having passed through the animal kingdoms to the human, he has arrived at the stage of Civilized Man? And, still with vast improvements and alterations necessary, does he continue to pass through numberless incarnations, evolving meanwhile, until . . .

'If you dream there much longer your tea will get cold. You'll feel much better after a cup.'

For the third time that evening I was brought down to earth with a shock, and, realizing that I had been literally dreaming on the after-deck while my indulgent host had been preparing tea, I entered the cosy cabin with guilt suffusing what I call my face. It is indeed strange, however, how the welcome odour of sardines and really hot tea banish one's higher thoughts and make life worth living once more!

Finding the tea-cloth pressed affectionately into my hand as soon as tea was over, I busied myself with the prosaic task of washing-up, surreptitiously placing the things as they got broken under one of the berths, while the Skipper bent the large jib. Maldon was now silhouetted with wonderful distinctness against a flaming sunset, the little church spire standing out like a minaret of the East against a cloud deeply tinged with crimson.

Clearly the chimes floated down to us again. Eight o'clock. From the fields beyond Mill Beach came the plaintive lowing of a solitary cow on her way home for the night. A slight mist was now rising over the canal at Heybridge, and several lights were beginning to twinkle in the gathering gloom.

'Hardly worth while getting any canvas up, there's not a breath of wind.'

The Skipper thoughtfully held the match up as he stood with his back to the cabin door and puffed vigorously at the newly-lit pipe. The flame burned motionless.

'I want to get down at least to the Stone to-night,' he added, 'so we'll see what the engine has to say about it.'

That engine had a lot to say about it. It began with an angry snort, a dull bark, and then took up its song in earnest, throbbing with vigorous, powerful life. The anchor was catted and our bowsprit was turned downstream once more, the dinghy following obediently in the race left by the propeller. And again on Northey that shrill cry rang out, but this time a mocking cry of disgust, while the throb and clatter of metal did its best to drown the sound.

'Jolly fine engine this. No trouble to start.'

The Skipper wiped his hands on a piece of oily waste, and his bulky form entered the cabin. On the eastern horizon, just beyond the trees of Osea, the moon was rising above the sea, paling the deep blue of the sky with her rich orange light. Presently the little jetty on the island was abeam, and the beweeded Barnacle, the old post to the east of the pier, glided by in solitary silence.

The tide had turned now, and we had the young flood against us. Not a word was spoken till the Stone was passed by and the lights of Tollesbury had twinkled distantly into view. The Skipper sat motionless and silent at the helm, his face in darkness, in the middle of which his trusty pipe burned like a red-hot coal. All around us nature seemed to be nodding; the birds were now silent; not a sound broke the stillness on the broad river but the rhythmic beat and echo of the engine.

'It's after eleven o'clock, young feller, and there isn't going to be any wind till morning, so I propose bringing up right here.'

The Skipper spoke in a whisper as though in fear of breaking up the stillness of the scene. The motor came to a final gasp and stopped, the anchor went overboard with a heavy splash, and the chain rattled out through the fair-lead till it was made fast to the bitts. Interest now centred itself round the cabin table, and an eager Primus noisily set to work to take the chill off coffee and other things.

Sometime later, with the supper things cleared, the Skipper and I sat in silence on the cabin-top, with our feet on the rail. The moon was now high up in the sky, and the distant lights of Tollesbury had gone out one by one. Not a breath stirred. The stars hung motionless in clusters, looking down upon the exquisite scene as a mother's gaze tenderly embraces her first-born.

'Don't believe in turning straight in on top of a heavy supper like that.'

I turned a deaf ear to the outrageous remark and

54

gazed with a sense of martyrdom at the dark line of the
trees ashore. Very faintly a clock somewhere chimed
the magic hour of twelve. It thrilled me. This was the
magic hour, when the whole world was changed, just for
a little while, when the fairies came out from the moss
and the ivy and danced in rings in the moonlight, and
a gnome sat in their midst playing exquisitely on delicate
pipes, and the owls, solemn and grotesque, sat on near-
by boughs and disapproved sedately. Possibly even in that
little spinney over there, where a light of some kind
seemed to dance through the slender trees. . . . I must
have uttered my thoughts aloud, for the Skipper took
the pipe from his mouth and peered intently at me.

'I don't think the National Fairies' Association,
Limited, has yet adopted Summer Time,' he said severely,
'so the show won't be for an hour yet. It's only eleven
o'clock really. I think I'd turn in, if I were you, and
sleep it off.' .

He *is* soulless!

. . . . .

'Bless my soul, if I don't drag him out in the morning
he'd lie there all day—till breakfast is ready!'

Vehemently protesting, I was gripped by my ankle
and dragged out of my warm berth on to the floor.
My aggressor—pardon, my host—departed backwards
through the doorway with a devilish grin on his face.
The linoleum on the floor was cold. My berth, for comfort, was ruined. I couldn't go to sleep again where I
lay, try as I would. There was no alternative. I took the
hint and got up.

It was a quarter-past seven. A keen sou'-west breeze

was blowing outside, and I began to wonder why men fit out ships and go all the way to the North Pole district in order to see what it's like to feel chilly. Thick rashers of bacon, bubbling eggs, slices of toast, marmalade, and hot coffee, however, modified my opinion of East Coast yachting, and even succeeded in making me temporarily forgive the Skipper for his harsh treatment.

When he had at last finished consuming thick slices of bread-and-marmalade, and I had ceased to wonder which would give out first, the loaf or the marmalade, the Skipper leisurely lit his pipe and significantly held the dish-cloth under my nose. I pretended to ignore it; but I defy anyone to sit in the cabin of a small yacht just after a meal, surrounded on all sides with unwashed saucers and plates and cups and things, with one's host waving the dish-cloth before one's face, and to maintain a perfect demeanour of innocence as to the next thing to be done. I failed dismally after a great effort, and so washed up. Washing-up and folding one's blankets between them come near to putting me off yacht cruising altogether.

Since it meant a good beat the whole way to windward, the Crouch was decided on as our destination to-day, and an hour later we were under way with all plain sail set. It was just about low water as we were abreast Bradwell and passed close to one of the big steamers laid up in the middle of the channel. There were eight of them, six steamers and two sailing-ships, gaunt, deserted, lonely objects of despair, their black sides showing red with rust, their rigging moaning dismally in the wind, the tide gurgling sluggishly round their massive rudders, and the mooring chains grinding and rasping with startling suddenness as the great hulls

56

turned slowly round to meet the young flood. They seem
uncanny—dead—as they lie there month after month,
yet teeming with life and sound of a bygone age, their
vast and intricate interiors resonant with the moan of
the wind through open doors and portholes, ventilator
shafts and hatches, and the incessant splash and wash of
the water outside.

But our little ship was taking all my attention as we
dashed past. Clear of Sales Point and heading for the
Bench Head buoy, we brought the wind abeam and lay
down to our channel plates, the occasional spray from
the weather side cutting across the cabin-top by the
mast and pattering into the foot of the mainsail. What
unbounded life! How she now quivered with energy
and strength, and how different she appeared under
these conditions compared with last night's moonlit
calm.

At this state of the tide there would not be quite enough
water over the Batchelor Spit at the entrance of the
Rays'n, the channel that runs up towards the mouth of
the Crouch River between the Buxey Sand and the
Dengie Flats. Thus we kept our sheets eased off and raced
on to the Bench Head buoy before close-hauling and
standing as near the wind as we could towards the
North Buxey buoy. There was a short, steep sea running
—the kind of sea that curls and breaks and meets one's
bow like the side of an upright wall, the kind that one
always finds in shallow seas and shoal-waters, where
the bottom also is uneven and the tides strong. Two
yachts were following us out of the Colne, both reefed
well down, while another cutter near the Buxey beacon
had hove-to and was tying in a reef. A Thames barge
ran past, probably bound down the Wallet to Harwich,

carrying full canvas and thrashing heavily against the foul tide.

'Fine going, old man!' the Skipper's voice shouted in my ear. 'But we'll have to have a reef ourselves soon.'

Crash, smash, clatter! As each steep sea encountered our weather bow it was broken into flying fragments that hurled themselves across the dripping deck and stung our faces. We were driving the boat for all she was worth through a dull, desolate scene, and she resented it.

The familiar Buxey beacon, with its eternal cormorant holding on against the onslaught of the wind, while the seas foamed and raced by 30 ft. below him, passed in a scurry of spray, and the West Buxey gas-buoy, appearing at intervals as a dark mark on the crested seas far away, could be seen to the sou-'east.

The sky was black to windward, and the sea, now a much darker shade of grey capped with white, hissing crests, was becoming heavier and more broken. Once or twice I had to ease the helm and allow the ship to luff into a sea for fear of the weight of water that would otherwise have come on deck. A reef became imperative.

Three minutes of breathless, arduous work, of clattering canvas and driving spray, of slippery decks and wild lurches, of dripping hands' and straining reef-points, then off we went again, our mizen and foresail stowed and a reef in the mainsail. It was blowing very hard now, and a yacht running out of the Crouch had dropped her mainsail and was continuing under her two headsails only. Out from the black cloud the squalls came down more and more viciously, till our lee-rail again became submerged, and the old yacht lay down and smothered herself in the seething spray.

'Look at our dinghy!'

I turned and caught sight of the little boat with her
bow in the air. For one instant she remained almost on
end, then the painter jerked taut and she followed
in a rush of foam. One or two green seas crashed over
our foredeck and ran along the waterways in cascades
over the counter. An old-fashioned yawl of about 12 tons
caught us up and passed us close to windward, her
long bowsprit burying itself in the seas and her square
forefoot appearing as she reared her deep head and
threw the spray high. It was a wild scene, typical of
the East Coast in early summer; dark-grey seas, steep,
curling, with long, white crests, following one another
with ceaseless energy; black, low, scurrying clouds above,
the wind shrieking through the tautened rigging and the
spindrift dashing occasionally into the straining mainsail and beating against our salt-stained faces. But such
is the very essence of yachting, the 'manly' part of the
game, the real test of ship and crew. It is comfortless,
savage, cold, dangerous, wearying, terrifying at times,
awe-inspiring, often needless and avoidable; yet there
is not a real sailor alive who does not enjoy putting
his own ship through such weather, if only to prove
that both she and he can stand it and come out
triumphant.

Half an hour later we were in still water, just laying
our course along the south shore of the Crouch, the
water quickly drying on our decks, and the sun showing
signs of peeping through a rift in the clouds. And when
we finally brought up off the end of Paglesham Hard
in the Roach River, a feeling of satisfaction stole over
us and made us forget the worst of it; and we forgot that
we were cold and wet and hungry as we snugged all the

dripping sails and halliards down and tidied up the old
and trusty vessel.

Next to Pin Mill, I believe Paglesham to be the
prettiest village on the East Coast accessible to the
yachtsman. Hidden in the midst of a little wood, it is
approached from the hard by a winding lane, and to a
stranger its presence is not suspected till a sudden turn
in the lane reveals its quaint cottages and their thatched
roofs. Thither we laid our tracks in search of butter and
new-laid eggs.

The wind was dying away as we got aboard, and the
evening was turning out fine. The little white horses had
disappeared now, and nothing but ripples remained,
and occasional cat's-paws flurried across the surface of the
water like the footprints of invisible water-sprites playing
hide-and-seek. Work had finished in the barge-repairing
shed at the head of the hard, and the men had returned
to their simple homes in the still of the evening. From
the hidden village distinctly came the sound of voices
and of a dog barking and the happy cries of children
playing on the Green. Our burgee was momentarily
flapping more languidly, and the incessant tap-tap of
the halliards gave way to periods of rest. The ebb was
sluicing past now, silently conveying thousands of tons
of water out into the North Sea.

'I think you said you'd get the tea ready to-night.'

The Skipper's insistent voice broke jarringly on my
itinerant thoughts and reminded me of a promise I
had made in a rash moment, hoping he'd forget all
about it. Therefore, with bowed head (partly due to lack
of headroom in the cabin) I entered to perform my duties.
I fully realized that we shouldn't have any tea unless I
did so.

'I've been thinking,' quoth my host to my undisguised astonishment as he later swilled the plates round with a disgracefully dilapidated mop, 'it wouldn't be a bad idea to take the last of this ebb down to Brankfleet Spit. It'll be handier for getting away in the morning.'

Thus, as the sinking sun was tinging the ripples behind us with caps of molten gold, our good ship once more turned her sturdy bowsprit seaward and began to glide down the Roach River on the last of the ebb. The dying breeze was pressing her white sails into those full, bellying curves that are so beautiful to the eye that sees and appreciates. Astern lay a wake of scintillating glory, while over Rochford way the sun was rapidly disappearing behind a group of Scotch firs, gauntly silhouetted against his crimson face.

'Keep a bit farther off the shore, old man.'

My host's patient tones struck shame into my heart and I pushed the helm gently to port, making a mental vow to keep my eye on the bowsprit in future. The breeze was hardly stirring the burgee now and the yacht scarcely had steerage way. There was but little ebb left, and as we drifted slowly down the last reach of the Roach towards Brankfleet Spit, where it joins the Crouch, night mysteriously drew her veil over the land.

'This'll do, I think. Let go!'

Splash, brrr-rrr-rr-r! The white hull turns round slowly as her anchor bites into the mud, and one by one the ghostly sails flutter down and are furled. The lights of Burnham twinkle in the distance, and the sound of a train with a healthy exhaust, climbing the Althorn bank, comes clearly to us. Then on Foulness, the other side, comes the plaintive lowing of some cows as they stumble homeward in the darkness. On one side Civilization; on the other the Simple Life; below, a cross between the two—the Skipper frying steak over a Primus.

We did not rise with the lark. I cannot believe that the famous early riser of the ornithological tribe would stay in bed till 10.15 a.m. We had intended getting up 'really early,' having a nice dip, a row in the dinghy, a little walk ashore, and, in fact, all those things that one feels one ought to do in the early, soulless hours of the morning—the night before. But we did get up, which is something, and we got under way within two hours of our rising, while a gentle sou'-westerly air wafted us out to the West Buxey buoy. We had, however, lost our tide. The flood was pouring up the coast and into all the numberless creeks and dykes and channels in the coast and filling up the narrow waterways that, at high water, separate the numerous islands that form the county of Essex.

So, with plain sail set, we just stemmed the floor in the Rays'n, but the wind began to fail and we slowly drifted astern. The sun, however, overcome by that curiosity that would almost seem to belie his sex, peeped from behind the clouds to see whither the wind have gone and gave us, in place of it, a gentle air from south-east. The old ship sluggishly gathered way while we stirred our lazy limbs and paid out the drooping sheets, the fairy-like music commenced at the bow in a gentle crescendo and rose to a steady melody as the breeze strengthened.

'Different here now, from yesterday.'

The Skipper was lying at full length on the foredeck, his head resting in his hands and his feet hanging over the rail, while large smoke rings issued from his mouth. That is his favourite attitude, and when thus he is not

a brilliant conversationalist. My remark, therefore, did
not receive applause.

The Buxey beacon was passing but slowly off to starb'd,
and we could see the swirl of water as it flowed past the
decaying post. The wind was failing again, and the boom
lifted and fell lazily, and the staysail hung motionless
over the inert form of the owner of the boat.

'We're drifting back.'

Slowly the old beacon was passing again in the
opposite direction. Bleak and ugly, like one of the old
French railway semaphores, it was slipping ahead of
us again, while the solitary cormorant sat on its top
and mocked us grotesquely. Around us on the oily water
lay several white sails. One or two were moving and the
faint sound of their auxiliary motors came to us.

Half an hour went by and no wind came. The beacon
was half a mile ahead of us again. The Skipper lifted his
head sleepily and yawned.

'What about some engine?' he suggested lazily.

Across the water a dark line was approaching from
the shore.

'There's a breeze coming, so don't fret about that
engine.'

The Skipper lay back relieved, and the boom slowly
gybed over, the headsails filled and once more the
dinghy began to run after the yacht, talking the while.
The air, coming from due west, increased in little puffs,
and before long we were beating against a stiff breeze
towards the Nass beacon at the entrance to Mersea
Quarters. With three other yachts bound the same way
there followed a glorious beat against the gathering
tide into Mersea Quarters, where we let go at the head
of Virley Creek against the old striped fishery beacon.

63

About noon the next day the old *Bint* lay once more on her moorings opposite the club house at Heybridge. Her sails were now stowed, and her owner was reluctantly making fast the last tier round the mainsail. On the cabin table a railway time-table lay open at the page on which read: 'Up trains, Maldon East and Liverpool Street.' The mate, with shaven chin and stiff collar, was tragically hauling in the dinghy's painter bit by bit, while his dripping hands ran affectionately along it and cleared it of the clinging weed.

And far away, from the other side of Northey, came that old familiar call. But this time in vain. For the short holiday was over. Naught but happy memories now remained.

IV

The Silent Creeks

THAT was not the way to sail a barge-yacht through a short chop, and well I knew it. But the ebb had just set in, and there would not be any too much water left in the maze of creeks above Hamford Water by the time I should get there.

With her weather chine 8 inches or so out of the water and the weather lee-board slashing at the tops of the seas as they pounded against her flat section, *Swan* continued in her frantic, headlong career while Dovercourt, with the long breakwater and the solitary beacon at the end, slipped by and passed astern.

A friend's white cutter-yacht was heading in for Harwich with the fresh southerly wind behind him, his dinghy standing nearly on end. She looked a fine sight with the mass of silver foam pouring away from her bows and the big jib and staysail ballooned out in startling whiteness against the dull sky. I waved to him as he passed through my wake.

'You'll have her over if you aren't damn careful!'

The words floated down to me as the distance between us rapidly increased, but I caught the note of scorn that told of an inborn hatred of barge-yachts and of consolation for fools who drive about in them as though they were aeroplanes.

But I knew *Swan*; not since I was *so* high, but well

65

enough to know that there was no need to worry about her going clean over until the weather chine was quite 18 inches out of the water. Slim and clean-lined, with very little chine and hardly a straight line anywhere, the little 6-tonner had been built in '97 at Chiswick, and was reputed to be the fastest barge-yacht round the coast; and she liked to prove it. Both her inboard lee-boards, steel plates that worked in mahogany cases like two centreboards against the shrouds, were down, and she was smashing her quixotic way over the short seas as though bent on showing what she could do.

Like a dinghy, she was wrenching at her helm, and if she were not constantly checked from rounding up or yawing off she would have run round in circles. Sailing such a boat on a course is a whole-time job and does not allow 'spells' with the tiller pegged. Restive and excited, she banged into hollows over which a heavy displacement boat would have passed gracefully, and her motion had already caused cooking utensils and stoves, the riding light and spare fenders to become mixed up into an unholy mess in the long, narrow fo'c'sle.

But as Stone Point at last came abeam and the Pye Sands stood between us and the seas coming round the Naze, the swell died down and nothing but wavelets remained. The wind, too, was dropping imperceptibly, and the steady rustle at the forefoot sounded peaceful in comparison with the noisy pounding and crashes of driven spray that had been our lot since leaving Harwich Harbour.

Swan appeared relieved at the sudden change, and as she heeled again to a last mild gust she whisked up Hamford Water while the red buoy at the mouth of Walton Creek bubbled past, nodding his beweeded head

66

as if to say, 'Oh, all right. Don't come up here if you
don't want to!' And the row of withies that stood against
the edge of Horsey Island waved to us as though they
themselves were surprised that any self-respecting yacht
should prefer to go up Hamford Water for the night
instead of the more congenial surroundings of the Twizzle
and Walton itself.

The only beacon that remained neutral was the dear
old thing with the can set jauntily on his head. I like that
beacon. He is the one I usually run into when trying
to make Walton Creek on a dark night. A canny withy,
indeed, which has suffered much!

But to-night I wanted solitude. The Twizzle, with
its small crowd of yachts, the dinghies flitting here and
there with vociferously happy crews; the congenial
club house, with its crowded rooms and laughter and
smoke-filled bar; the ladies' room, with its chattering
occupants that seemed to all the world like a poultry
run wherein a terrier has been let loose, and the streets
and prom of the 'attractive watering-place' itself . . .
No. To-night I had a lot of writing to do, and it was one
of those pitifully rare occasions when the so-called 'urge
to write' did not require to be dragged forth by the
scruff of its unwilling neck and compelled by mental
cudgelling to produce, produce, and then some.

The sedge-covered flats of Horsey Island were slipping
by close to windward, and the lonely cries of wildfowl
were carried across them by the dying breeze. Once a
flock of redshank sailed across our bows on a level with
the burgee, the swish of their wings passing like a gentle
whisper in the trees. And Kirby Creek opened out,
revealed itself abeam, then closed up once more and
passed astern; just an opening in the sedge bank wherein

67

one saw a twisting stream of water leading to—where? One could imagine it as a smugglers' haunt that became the scene of silent grim activity on dark nights.

But my frolicsome little companion was not thinking of these things of the past. This breeze was all she cared about, and as an extra and final puff bent the taller heads of the long sedge grass towards us, she heeled winsomely, and scurried ahead, dragging the protesting pram-dinghy after her as a mother leads her child across a crowded street. And Pewit Island to leeward, with its deserted, winding creek leading in towards the dim hills that stood on the mainland past the quaint factory that seems almost derelict, passed astern gradually, and before us Hamford Water broke up into two narrow channels.

There would, by now, be very little water in the one to starboard, and although with both her plates and drop-rudder hauled up, *Swan* would float in twelve modest inches of moisture, one could not beat to windward thus. Into the narrow neck of water that opened out to port, therefore, I shot the boat, and in frantic movements, susceptible to every touch of the helm, the little barge began to beat up in ridiculously short boards between the mud of Skipper's Island and the desolate sedge and mud-bank that is marked on the chart as another island. Down this narrow gulley the ebb was running fast, emptying the expanse of shallow water that leads finally up to Beaumont's Quay. But each board brought us nearer to the narrow opening that would suddenly appear in the mud to starboard and lead between the two islets into the shallow mere beyond, wherein I could find a comfortable, soft berth for the night.

On either side the mud was revealing itself in naked simplicity, and a continuous hiss came from it as the tide receded; whilst here and there little jets of water spurted up where tiny creatures lived and throve. Then the idea of the little terrier let loose amongst the hens recurred, and my thoughts reverted, in some mysterious fashion, to the congenial club house but two miles away. . . .

The sun had just set behind vague clouds that had refused him one last look at the world before retiring for the night, and darkness was waiting to descend upon us. The autumn air was chilly now, and I beat my hands to restore their vanished circulation. Across a level bank of mud the trees on Skipper's Island were silhouetted against the darkening sky in the east. They stood clustered together as though afraid of the oncoming gloom, gaunt arms spread out towards one another, heads nodding sleepily, the grass at their feet already drowsy and inert. A faint air passed through their still branches, and their sigh came delicately across the intervening mud and water, a sigh of contentment that a child makes when it is on the verge of Dreamland.

A gentle, soft scraping brought me back to earth suddenly. The steel lug on the starboard lee-plate was lifting. Pushing the helm down with that portion of the anatomy so apt for the purpose, I grasped the tackle and hauled up the plate. For a moment *Swan* hung in stays tantalizingly, then her tanned foresail filled aback, and with one sweep she had slewed round and was off towards the other bank, pointing almost downstream. But in a minute she was again under proper control and beating lazily up against the ebb.

At last the tiny creek that led between the two islets appeared to starboard, and in a minute the slim little barge was chuckling up between two steep banks

69

that closed in upon her until there seemed not room to pass another vessel of her size, should we meet one. But the chance was unlikely, for few cabin yachts get up as far as this, except at high water, and no open boats would be about here at this time in the evening. The place seemed utterly deserted, and as the rugged outline of the banks on either side slid silently by I could not help thinking what an ideal place it would be to ambush a visiting yacht and hold her to ransom. . . . Once a number of fowl took to the air from the grass close to leeward, and their sudden advent startled me as though a rifle bullet had passed through my mainsail!

As quickly as it had narrowed the creek opened out again, and revealed before me a dim expanse of water on which ripples chased one another amongst tall grass that appeared here and there above the placid surface. It was now too dark to see the quay at the head of the creek, but one or two lights told where the cottages that looked over the water at high tide stood near the wharf. There is a faint channel that leads right up to Beaumont's Quay, but I did not know it, and although I saw one stray withy apparently out in the middle I knew not which side of it the deeper water lay.

A sudden scraping reminded me of the lee-boards again, and I hauled the starboard one right up. The tackle of the other I held in my hand, with the plate but half down. Hardly a sound broke the stillness of the on-coming night. The wind had almost died right away, and only when a cat's-paw kissed the tanned mainsail did the dinghy reveal its presence by murmuring contentedly. I looked back at my wake. It was smooth off the weather quarter, and a line of bubbles was rising to the surface from under the rudder. We were making frightful leeway.

'HARDLY A SOUND BROKE THE STILLNESS OF THE ONCOMING NIGHT'

Then she stopped. It was no use trying to get any
nearer to the quay now. She was aground for the night.
So was the dinghy. Never mind, it was quite a nice place,
and, being a barge, she would sit upright. I jumped over
in my sea-boots into a few inches of water and planted
the anchor a few yards away. Then the canvas was stowed
and everything on deck made shipshape.

It was quite dark now, and while the Primus stoves
were left to boil water and heat up a typical stew, and
the light from the little corner cabin lamp cast beams
through the rectangular portlights, I sat on the cabin-
top and listened to the sounds of the night.

A train was pulling out from Frinton Station. A dog
heard it and barked. A curlew, from somewhere over
Skipper's Island, called his mate and got no reply.
Wrong number or wrong mate. Voices were coming
faintly from the direction of the quay, and a motor-
horn broke the stillness of the Kirby road. And the mud
all round was hissing as the last of the tide receded from
sight, leaving a thin, tortuous rivulet that trickled down
the middle of the creek a few feet from the yacht's bow.

The night grew colder as the stars appeared one by
one, and above the uncertain marshes through which
we had threaded our way a mist was rising, ghostlike,
unfolding its white coils over the damp grass and making
the scene vaguer and more mysterious than ever.

It was eerie and lonely out here, and somehow every
sound ceased, as though the rest of the world had
suddenly been cut off, and I instinctively pulled the collar
of my jacket up and slipped my hands under the lapels.
A dead, uncanny silence reigned over everything. And
now the mist was around us, blotting out everything
but the dark mass of the dinghy as it rested on the mud

73

and the four yellow beams of light that escaped through the portlights.

An owl hooted with startling suddenness from a far-off spinney. The queer, raucous voice rose to a hideous shriek like a soul in agony, and seemed to rend the fog with its outlandish cacophonous horror. A screech-owl, unholy prophet of untold miseries. . . . But I became aware of a slight odour that brought me violently to my senses again, causing me to leave my hard seat precipitately and dash into the warm cabin. That stew had just begun to catch.

And I spent the rest of the night, before turning in for good, in the warmth of the cabin, while the screech-owl hooted itself hoarse in vain to the sound of my portable typewriter.

But what a change next morning! The early sun, glad to be about again, was glinting on the dew-covered deck, and what had been the previous night murky stretches of uncertain mud was now an expanse of mirror-like water. Hardly a breath stirred, and the reflections of the trees were reproduced faithfully on the placid surface. From the wharf a barge was drifting down, light, her familiar topsail and big mainsail set in the hope of catching any draught that was going. It was just high water, and the islands that had last night appeared as high banks of mud with gaunt sedge on the top, now seemed to be flat fields of coarse grass out of which grew lonely, rotten stumps and broken withies.

The barge drifted nearer, her reflection playing idly before the bluff bows, and her dinghy following on the end of a heavy painter that drooped in the middle to the surface. As the stately old vessel glided past within a few yards of *Swan*, the old Skipper left the wheel and

74

stood against the rail, hands in pockets, surveying the unfamiliar little barge-yacht.

'Nice mornin'.'

I agreed, and begged to ask his opinion on the chance of getting any wind to-day. Appeal for a person's opinion if his heart is to be won.

'Aw, yus. Nice breeze'll come up from th' southward later on.'

I thanked him, and watched his little white terrier pacing the deck at twenty-five miles an hour.

'Yap, yap, yap!' was *his* opinion on the weather, strange barge-yachts and life in general. Poor wee bow-wow, it may be the best one, for all I know!

And when they had gone and only the masts and patched tanned sails appeared over the sedge grass of the unnamed islet, I stripped in the well, paused for a deep breath on the cabin-top, and then dived into the limpid depths of the creek. And everywhere silence reigned, the silence of big open spaces, of Nature at her best, of the—creeks.

V

The Voice of the Shingle

THE cool night wind was murmuring softly across the marshes that stretched unseen towards Tollesbury. As the little pram-dinghy was urged forward with rhythmic jerks of the short paddles the water rustled before its transom bow, and the wash ran in a series of ripples that chased one another along the edge of the mud. Astern, the few lights of West Mersea shimmered on the mudflats on which the black forms of boats lay with their masts at drunken angles.

A tall withy, festooned with weed, loomed up out of the darkness, and Hugh had to ship one paddle hurriedly as the beacon brushed along the dinghy's side. It made a scraping sound and the stillness was broken by a scuttle from the forward thwart and a crescendo of indignant comments from the third member of our party.

'Dry up, Scottie!' said Hugh, as he put his weight into the oars again. 'Keep still, old man, or you'll capsize us.'

But Scottie was true to his Aberdonian origin, and not to be so easily shushed. Until we had passed Packingmarsh Island and rowed out into the Quarters, he stood in the bow with his paws on the forward transom, sniffing the variety of smells that was coming from the heaps of sun-dried cockle shells on the shore, and giving an occasional bark.

76

Seated in the sternsheets of the 8-ft. pram, with a suit-case on my knees, I was wondering whether Hugh was wise or not in bringing his Scottish terrier with him, when his voice interrupted my profound debate.

'The wind's westerly to-night, Maurice,' he said, 'and that's a fair wind for us. The forecast said "easterly winds"; I reckon we ought to get round to Harwich to-night if we can, for it may come easterly to-morrow. Ah, there she is.'

As we slid alongside the little white barge-yacht, Scottie leapt on to her deck, and the sudden release of his weight caused my end of the cranky pram to ship water. But a friendly muzzle with a moist tongue was thrust in my face as I clambered aboard, and I knew he was going to be one of the crew without doubt. Scottie was the kind of dog that made you feel you couldn't do without him somehow.

Seamew was a 6-ton barge-yacht of uncertain vintage and somewhat box-like appearance with iron lee-boards pivoted on the sides and iron guides to keep them from swinging away from the ship. It was said that many years before she had had her bottom doubled. My friend Hugh had bought her at West Mersea only a few weeks previously, and as he lived not far from Lowestoft it was his intention to take her round to the Broads the first available week-end.

I was not without a boat at the time, for I still had *Swan*, another small barge of a slimmer, less angular type, but with her lee-boards working in cases, and I supposed it was my ownership of a similar type of craft that induced him to invite me. At any rate, the idea of a coastal passage in a small barge-yacht which was not by any means seaworthy appealed to me as a

77

thoroughly sporting venture—with someone else's boat at stake!

When I had said it seemed a longish passage, especially between Orford Haven and Lowestoft, for a 26-ft. flat-bottomed yacht with no ballast and (I was going to say) a rotten hull, my friend, who had owned one other boat only, a half-decked sailing-punt which had quietly filled and settled for life at moorings, had only laughed a careless laugh and declared, 'Why, the old hooker only draws 18 inches, and if you get caught out in a barge you just run her ashore!'

'Ashore?'

'Why yes, up the beach—anywhere. By the time she touches bottom there isn't enough water to float a jelly-fish, and the waves can't break!'

I had breathed a prayer that we should have no cause to try his theory, and let it go at that. He must have read somewhere that the skippers of the Thames spritsail barges sometimes let their big vessels take the ground on one of the more sheltered sands in the Estuary during a 'blow' to ensure a quiet night.

We stowed our gear in the cunningly contrived lockers of the overcrowded cabin and sat down to a meal of cold pie, while two black eyes set above a shaggy muzzle watched our every movement from the darkness of the cockpit. If one so much as glanced in the direction of the open doors two upright ears would drop simultaneously and an invisible tail thump on the floor-boards. I was glad now Hugh had brought him.

It was about ten o'clock when we set the mainsail and foresail—*Seamew* had no bowsprit and set only one headsail—and ran gently down the Quarters past the Nass beacon.

There was no cormorant on the drunken old post to-night, I noticed. I wondered, musingly as I sat at the tiller, where that black, gaunt bird had gone. The Nass beacon is so seldom without its sleek figurehead which turns an angular beak first one way and then the other as you drift past, that he seems to be part of the effigy. But to-night the beacon slipped past into the darkness astern, untenanted, and a solitary light winked far up the Blackwater.

The breeze was gradually taking off, and soon after midnight, when the loom of Colne Point was just visible to port, *Seamew* scarcely had steerage way through the water. The young flood had by now begun, and we were slowly but surely being carried back.

'No use drifting back, is there?' said Hugh, and we let go the hook on the edge of Colne bar and stowed the mainsail.

Half an hour later I lay in my bunk listening to the strange noises of a strange craft. A slight swell kept the boat rolling, and she rolled quickly, as all small barges will, rocking from side to side in a frenzy; then unaccountably remaining perfectly still and silent, but for the gurgle of bilge water, for perhaps ten seconds. A lurch would follow and the rapid rolling begin again. The bilge water sloshed back and forth, back and forth under the floor-boards, and every now and then one of the lee-boards would bang the side close to my head with a noise like a steam pile-driver. How Hugh slept through it was not only beyond my understanding, but it positively enraged me.

But I must have dozed, for I woke up once during the night and found *Seamew* still rolling. The noise of the bilge water sounded louder, and I put the back of

79

one hand on to the floor by my bunk. The water was not over the floor-boards, thank goodness, but a cold nose and a moist warm tongue on my wrist reminded me that Scottie was curled up on a mat on the floor. I went to sleep again fondling one of his ears.

'That forecast was right,' Hugh's voice was saying; 'the wind's easterly this morning.'

There seemed to be an alarming racket going on as I woke up. The Primus was roaring heartily in the cooking locker, and *Seamew's* antics of a few hours before had now become chronic. She was pitching and rolling, the lee-boards were thudding against the sides with frantic irregularity, the bilge water was washing back and forth with a sound like 'breakers ahead,' and the halliards, which we had forgotten to frap, or tie up, were clattering on the mast.

'I've got the kettle on for breakfast,' Hugh called out cheerily from the open doors. 'I'm just going to give the dog a run ashore if you don't mind getting breakfast ready.'

It was less than a quarter of a mile to the sandy point of land, and while I stirred the scrambled eggs in the saucepan and swore because the toast would catch, I could see my cheerful skipper giving his dog a run, as he called it, on the beach.

Judging from Hugh's attitude as he sat on the edge of the dinghy and tried to make the dog understand why he had been brought for a run ashore, it appeared to be a game of patience. Convinced that it was all a game, Scottie had laid a huge stone at his master's feet, and now sat looking up expectantly at him. The proverb 'you can take a horse to the pond, but you can't make him drink' came to mind, and I nearly burned the eggs through helpless merriment. Yet when Hugh returned, he said he couldn't see anything funny in it; the dog was simply pig-headed.

The breeze was comparatively fresh when we got the anchor aboard and stood out towards the Knoll buoy on the port tack. The sun appeared through a haze and glinted on a sea whose heaving surface was of that peculiar opaque and sandy green with streaks of light and dark shade and flashes of white where crests were breaking, that is so well portrayed in the sea-pieces of Van de Velde. Already some of the Brightlingsea fishing-smacks were on their trawling grounds beyond the bar, their mainsails triced up and spitfire jibs set half-way along their long bowsprits.

Seamew was bounding over the seas in the erratic and light-hearted manner of the small barge-yacht, her weather chine appearing as the waves passed under her and the tiller requiring both hands to keep her full and bye.

It was a dead-beat as far as Clacton, the ebb was with us, and we were not making bad headway. But the seas were becoming lumpy, and with no reef in the mainsail it was a ticklish business humouring the boat over some of the crests. If you luffed into them, the boat carried no way and stopped dead, only to pay off and meet the next sea on her beam, putting a terrific strain on her iron lee-boards. Some of the seas were steep enough to be a positive danger to a flat-bottomed boat which was carrying too much canvas.

'We ought to have a reef in,' I ventured once as our weather chine rose above the water and a sea hit our flat bottom with a jarring thump. But her proud owner only laughed in a care-free manner.

'Oh, she's doin' fine. It's the only way to get a barge

81   F

to wind'ard—to *drive* her. Besides, I reckon the wind'll take off this afternoon.'

But it did not, and in a nasty jump of a sea off Frinton we were forced to roll down a few turns on the mainsail. The main boom was fitted with the type of roller-reefing gear which is actuated by a wire unrolling from a reel at the forward end of the boom. This, of course, jammed, and caused us to curse it and each other with such volubility that we failed to notice how much ground we lost with wind and the young flood against us.

At last we rounded the Naze and were able to lay a course for Harwich Harbour. And when we brought up close to the beach inside Languard Point, convenient for slipping out the following morning, and Hugh took Scottie ashore to look for a lamp-post, I began to feel that small barge-yachts had their limitations when it came to making coastal passages.

You cannot drive them like a keel boat, and as soon as they show signs of carrying too much canvas you have to reef immediately, or sail with your teeth and the boat, so to speak, on edge. With a cheerful, reckless skipper like Hugh aboard and a boat with the unexpected tendencies of *Seamew*, I decided I should have to insist on considerably more caution for the remainder of the passage, even though I was only the mate!

Sunday was cold, with a pale look about the sun and a slight haze in the sky that gave it an uncertain, steely tinge. The wind was blowing somewhat fresh from a little south of east and bringing a swell with it into the harbour that made breakfast aboard *Seamew* a precarious affair. One sudden lurch sent Hugh's plate into his lap, and his expression as he retrieved what was left of his

82

fried kipper was such a study of injured annoyance that I failed to stop a cup of tea from following the plate.

That cabin was not large enough to hold all of us for the next few minutes, and Scottie wisely retreated to the cockpit, where he laughed at us with hysterical barks.

'This wind'll just about let us fetch round Orfordness,' Hugh observed, with his usual recklessness, when he had subsided and eaten my kipper while I was busily clearing up the mess. 'And once round the Ness we'll carry it abeam to Lowestoft. And, boy,' he added in the manner of a talkie fan, 'we'll sure show 'em what a cute lil' barge can do.'

I managed to induce him to roll in one reef in the mainsail before starting, and by the time we had worked slowly out against the second half of the flood-tide and slipped over the Platter Sands, where a confused sea treated *Seamew* as though she were more of a box than her owner would admit, we were glad to have taken the precaution.

There was still a strong tide running against us, and in spite of a fresh wind we seemed to make slow progress past Felixstowe front with its pier and row of white beach-huts, and the mouth of the Deben opened out slowly between the sand-dunes on the Felixstowe ferry side and the Bawdsey cliffs. But before the coastguard cottages near Orford Haven came into view, where the Ore River meets the sea amid a dreaded nest of shingle banks, worse indeed for their uncertainties and dangers than Woodbridge Haven, the ebb set in, and the low-lying land began to slip by perceptibly.

'The wind's backed a bit,' said Hugh once. 'There's Orfordness lighthouse and I can't quite point it.'

83

The black-and-white striped pillar of the lighthouse appeared over the horizon a little to windward of our forestay. Making as much leeway as she was, *Seamew* could never weather the Ness, and we should have to make a tack out to sea.

The wind was freshening by degrees and *Seamew* was pounding badly at times, occasionally getting a sickening thump under her weather chine from a heaped-up sea. When we had got past the slight lee afforded by the Whiting Bank the seas were all much bigger and had to be carefully manœuvred. The beach, known here as Shinglestreet, looked particularly desolate as we closed in on it, for there was nothing to see but miles of wind-swept shingle with here and there a patch of coarse grass, an occasional hut and, in the distance, a long line of gaunt telegraph poles.

'Once we've weathered the Ness,' Hugh called out with a forced gaiety, 'we'll have the wind free, and we can put into Southwold if it gets too uncomfortable.'

Holding on to the cockpit coaming as the barge banged into the hollows and threw herself over the crests with a wild motion like an enraged mule, I wondered how much comfort there was to be had already. But the sight of Scottie, curled up on his mat under the cabin table, uncomplaining and obviously prepared to go wherever his master would take him, reassured me.

The roar of the seas as they broke on the shore a hundred yards to leeward in an unending line of heaving white foam was sinister, as though the Fates only waited for us to round the Ness before mocking us for our foolishness.

'Better not get too close to a lee-shore,' I ventured once, when the noise of the seas and the scream of the
84

shingle as the spent fury rushed down the beach in a sullen torrent of speckled foam almost deafened us.

'Oh, all right. Lee-oh!'

Seamew swung into the wind, her canvas flogging, hovered for one moment as a sea broke against her bow, dropped suddenly into the hollow beyond, and paid off on to the new tack. Then began a long plunge away from the dreaded shore. I glanced into the cabin and caught sight of two black eyes watching me with a puzzled look, while beneath them a long nose, ending in a shiny-black button, was flanked on either side by a row of whiskers that bristled out with an air of intense indignation. Scottie was standing up, for the sudden change of angle had upset him, and he wondered if that was all right and as his master intended.

'All right, Scottie, lie down.'

The ears dropped quickly at my voice, and in a minute he had made the best of the new conditions and settled once more under the table.

Once again on the starboard tack we pointed down the coast, the only sail in sight. But the wind had backed still more, and to our chagrin we found we could scarcely lay the town of Aldeburgh, nestling under a hill four miles ahead. The seas were nearly all breaking now, and once or twice *Seamew* gave a lurch to leeward that stressed a dangerously small limit of safety.

The Aldeburgh Ridge buoy passed slowly abeam to seaward, appearing every now and then against the hard, wave-topped line of the horizon, like a policeman's helmet above a surging crowd of people.

'We'll have to reef again,' Hugh called out as a sudden lurch nearly threw us on to the lee-coaming. 'I can hardly hold her!'

I took a fearful glance at the deserted shore but a cable's length away, and then we worked hurriedly to roll some more turns in the main boom. When we had finished, there was the equivalent of three reefs rolled in the mainsail and the lee shore was appreciably closer.

As we gathered way again, Scottie came into the cockpit, wagging his tail and whining. A glance into the cabin showed what had troubled him.

'Good Lord! The water's over the cabin floor.'

Hugh looked at the breakers under our lee.

'This pounding's straining her,' he said. 'But I've got to keep her going, old man. Will you try to pump her out?'

The semi-rotary pump in the well would not suck at first, and I spent many minutes trying to prime it with a mug of sea-water. At last it started to throw out absurd jets of water, and for some time I sat working the handle. But soon it sucked air, although the water was washing about in the cabin up to the level of the lee-berth, and I found I could not pump out any more while she was sailing, as the pipe led to one side of the keel amidships, and, of course, was uncovered as she heeled. It should have had a pipe leading to each bilge, with a two-way cock.

Without any warning a harder squall than usual laid the boat over until her lee-rail was submerged, and as she hovered in this position, a sharp snap forward was followed by a ripping of canvas as the mainsail suddenly unrolled in a huge bag.

For one moment I felt certain *Seamew* was going right over, but with the helm hard down she sprang into the wind, while the mainboom with its folds of canvas swept across the well and threatened to brain us.

'The reefing wire's gone!' was all Hugh said, and for a moment we looked at one another in dismay.

That wretched bit of wire which wound the boom round on its reel had parted and all the reefs had unrolled. Like nearly all mainsails made for roller reefing, it had no row of reef-points and cringles for such an emergency, and somehow or other we had to get those turns in again before the barge went ashore.

I said as much to Hugh, but his theory came to mind and he pointed to leeward, where the seas were sweeping up the beach and returning, only to attack again in a smother of white foam with an unceasing roar.

'We could sail her straight in,' he shouted, 'and beach her. She's a barge and wouldn't——'

'Don't be a——' I replied savagely, and meant it. There was nothing for it but to let go the anchor on its full scope and pray that the cable would not part. As I veered it out the chain felt very small and rusty as though it would never stand the strain, but the anchor seemed to take a hold, and there we lay with our sails loosely furled, perhaps a hundred yards off the beach, pitching wildly and snubbing with horrible crashes on the cable as the boat's head rose to a crest.

With the little barge jumping about as she was, it was no easy task to roll the mainboom with the sail neatly round it by hand, but in due course we had about eight turns in it, and the ends lashed so that it could not unroll again. Nor, incidentally, could we put in any more reefs unless we had the sail down again and untied the lashings.

Meanwhile, the wind had increased, and from the hard, cold look of the horizon, which was broken by a dark, heaving line of crests, it was obviously going to

87

blow, and blow *hard*, from the east'ard. And no boat should be on this coast with a gale in that quarter. The afternoon was far advanced by now, and it would be dark in an hour or two.

No harbour lay farther north nearer than Southwold, some thirteen miles; but that place, with its narrow entrance, its shallow bar on which the seas would be breaking, and the strong cross-set of the tide between the piers, would be a death-trap in the darkness. There was nothing for it but either to run all the way back to Harwich and leave the boat, say, at Pin Mill until next week-end, or run into Orford Haven and go up to Slaughden Quay, near Aldeburgh.

It seemed cruel to think that this very sheltered river was even now but a quarter of a mile beyond that deadly shingle beach which was screaming in derision at our puny efforts, while the entrance was still some seven miles away.

'If she won't claw off,' Hugh said in a queer high-pitched voice, as we set the mainsail once more, 'we can at least sail her hard for the beach, and a wave would help us get her well up. I've always heard that a small barge . . .'

But I did not wait to hear more of his pet theory and began to haul in the straining cable. The idea of deliberately putting a 6-ton barge-yacht on to that beach on which 6-foot seas were bursting into wind-driven spray seemed too mad to contemplate. Of course, if we could not possibly thresh out against this rising wind, or the mainsail blew away and she just went ashore, then it mean a jump for our lives and Heaven help the boat. She would be filled with shingle and her planking strewn along the beach in a few hours. One way and another we had got ourselves into a pretty fix, and I hadn't as much faith as I should have liked in the boat or her skipper to get out of it.

As soon as we had the anchor catted and the foresail set, *Seamew* heeled over and showed that, reefed down as she was, she still needed the most careful handling. The seas smashed against her weather bow, driving her head off, and as the squalls laid her over, the water thudded heavily under her flat bottom and shook her whole fabric. For an hour we plunged and tossed into the seas, drenched with spray, shaken and—apprehensive. The sight of the breakers under our lee and the continuous roar dinning in our ears made one's heart turn to water, and after the first three tacks, when it appeared we had not gained a yard, I began to experience a dull fear, an unreasonable fear that would not be stilled by thoughts that *of course* the little boat could claw off. But I was frightened and felt that Hugh secretly shared my feelings.

The cabin floor was awash, and the berth cushions had long been soaked beyond hope. Scottie had vacated his mat, which was floating back and forth across the floor, and now stood on his hind legs, clutching the cockpit coaming with his fore-paws, his grizzly muzzle facing the wind.

There was an air of defiance about his little rigid body, a show of unquenchable spirit of the Highlands that attracted me, and when he snapped savagely at a dash of salt water that flew into his face, I felt that if he could treat the elements like that, why shouldn't we? It put heart into us, and we drove the little barge harder, oblivious of her straining timbers and complaining hull.

At last we had opened out the Ness once more and were able to ease the sheets a little. With steep, green seas leaping up at her port side, *Seamew* scurried back along the coast towards the mouth of the Ore River. It was already getting dusk, and it seemed a toss-up whether we could pick our way between the deadly shoals into the Haven before it became too dark to make out the leading marks or to attract a pilot.

The sea was taking on a darker shade as the light began to fail, and the bigger seas looked black in their hollows beneath the white of their crests. *Seamew*, reeling and lurching, staggered on, her wake hissing out from under her broad transom and colliding with the waves as they raced across it.

'The dinghy's filled, Maurice.'

I had almost forgotten the pram, but the Skipper's remark revealed our little boat towing with only the forward transom showing. Luckily, we had lashed the paddles in it, but I gave anxious glances at the bar-taut painter watching for signs of its parting.

At last, in the gathering dusk, we approached Orford Haven. Against the dark line of the beach and the pine-trees beyond we could see the line of white that marked the entrance—a boiling cauldron of water wherein, here and there, shingle banks rose up like the backs of whales, and were smothered again and again. It was a sight that would test the courage of the bravest, for as we rushed towards the place it seemed as though we were heading for certain destruction.

'My God, there *isn't* any entrance!'

Hugh's ejaculation was understandable, but I had been in once before and, scared though I was, I believed that I might be able to feel out the channel where *Seamew's* light draught could take her. But I wished fervently that one of the pilots would come out and take us in.

90

Already the sound of the seas was getting louder, with a deadly roar.

'Look, there's somebody waving!'

I followed the direction of his hand and saw to my relief a dim figure, looking absurdly small on the beach, waving a flag. It was one of the pilots, and he was going to 'flag' us in as it was too bad on the bar for their boat to put off.

On we swept, with wind and seas chasing us like the fiends of hell, our swamped pram surging along on the end of an already stranded painter. Acting as a drogue, perhaps that little dinghy was saving us from being pooped—swamped by a sea breaking over our open cockpit. But the pilot—where was he? He'd gone; no, there he was—waving again—God, which way? Port? *Not* through that mass of breakers! Heavens, that's a shoal; no, he's waving again—starboard.

'There's a big sea coming, hold on!'

Hugh was looking astern while I wrestled with the tiller. No time to look astern; I can hear it roaring, roaring, coming on, mounting high, tumbling over, the shingle screaming in our ears on either side; mad, mad, that was it, the whole place mad with fury at losing us—no, *they* are only jeering at us. Those hell fiends might get us yet. We are only now over the bar—what's he doing now? Why doesn't he *wave?* Oh God, which way? There's white water all round us.

With an angry roar the comber is breaking close astern of us. Water on deck, running over the coamings, boiling, roaring, cascading. *Seamew* being carried wildly towards the shore, little Scottie savagely snapping at the spray. She's broaching-to—I can't hold her; this tiller will break if she doesn't—ah! She's on her course again,

91

and the pilot's waving us to starboard—why doesn't he stand *higher*? I can't see him, it's getting too dark against those trees . . . never mind, we're in the river now.

And as we passed out of the turmoil, gybed to starboard and stemmed the sluicing ebb that poured through the Narrows, I could have sworn I heard the shingle give a prolonged screech of anger at our escape.

Through heaven-sent smooth water we sailed slowly with the wind abeam, its force broken into occasional gusts by the high bank of deserted shingle that separated us from the fury of the sea. Where the channel divided at Havergate Island we turned to port and entered the narrow and tortuous Butley Creek, where willy-waws chased one another across the placid surface and our wash broke on the mud on either side.

An hour later, with the cabin partially dried and a hot meal eaten, I went on deck to bail out the pram dinghy. *Seamew* lay quietly at anchor, with the mud of the narrow creek within a few yards on either side, while the gusts of wind roared through her rigging and rustled through the long sedge grass on the bank. From the direction of Shinglestreet was coming a continuous booming sound, the sullen anger of the sea in mighty conflict with the shore.

And when, later, I took the pluckiest member of the crew ashore in the dinghy and felt his warm tongue against my hand as I sat on the grass in the darkness, I could not help gazing back at the little white barge, whose round port-holes showed bright from the cabin lamp, and wondered what would have become of us had we tried to push on to Southwold in her on this blustering night.

The roar of the shingle gave me an idea.

92

VI

Rain and Wind

THE glass was very low. I tapped it gently with the knuckle of my finger and it dropped still farther. With the wind in the east it probably foretold a sudden shift sooner or later, followed by a good deal of it. A snug anchorage would be the thing for the night, and with the probability of the blow coming from its old quarter, south-west, where it had stayed on and off for over a month, I decided to run up the Stour and bring up under the lee of Wrabness cliff.

As I stood propped against the cabin table while the water dripped from my oilskins on to the floor, *Storm* continued her way with helm pegged, her tanned sails bellying under the scurries that came down from the east.

She was an ideal single-handed cruiser, a 7-ton cutter built on the lines of a Leigh bawley, 26 ft. overall, 9 ft. beam, and drawing but 3 ft. 3 in., with no centre-board, and she was fitted with a single-cylinder $3\frac{1}{2}$-h.p. Kelvin motor. She and I had formed an intimate friendship that we little imagined would be cruelly severed within a tragic year.

I closed the door behind me and sat for a moment on the wooden engine cover. The sky was leaden, and across the slate-coloured furrows of the water, flecked here and there with caps of white, the teeming rain drove in sheets, and cat's-paws hurried after one another across the tops of the waves for all the world like the footprints of invisible sprites at play. It was late in the season, and though five o'clock had barely struck, darkness had already placed her clammy finger over the obscure scenery.

Away ahead, a mile farther down Sea Reach, a few lights twinkled in the indistinct mass that was Harwich, and dimly the red eye of the Guard buoy solemnly winked as though egging *Storm* on. A pale star off the port bow grew and the dark mass of the old pilot-boat *Lena* that used to be moored there in those days slithered by in silence, her riding light casting an unnatural glow over the streaming decks. Born in the middle 'sixties at the yard of the famous Fifes, *Lena* was a typical example of the old-time racing yacht of about 40 tons. She has since been sold out of the pilot service and now reposes as a house-yacht at Pin Mill.

Soon the spherical buoy marking the end of Shotley Spit washed dimly into view, sheets were eased and *Storm* altered her course up the Stour, while the rain pelted on the back of my oilskins and trickled down my sea-boots into the well. The ebb-tide that had helped the yacht down from Pin Mill was now against her, but the squally easterly wind was driving her ably up against it at a steady five and a half knots. It was but an hour's run at this rate to Wrabness, and with the certainty of meeting no traffic above Parkeston I did not bother about the side-lights, but kept a hurricane lamp lighted and obscured in the well ready for use. Not a single light showed ahead when the arc lamps over Parkeston Quay had once dropped astern, and it seemed as though *Storm* and I sailed together into an unknown world of pitchy night. The squalls were, however, taking off as the rain increased. The pull on the helm was growing less insistent, and the steady rush of parting waters at the forefoot was lessening imperceptibly.

Then the wind went altogether and down came the rain. The yacht lost her way as though she were bewildered by the intense darkness, while the rain fell on the oily water and hissed on the decks, trickled in miniature cataracts through the scuppers and poured off the limp mainsail in unending torrents. With the ebb still running there was nothing to do but to start the engine and make sure of reaching Wrabness to-night. Kelvin went off with the usual kick on the starting handle, and to the accompaniment of its methodical, muffled throb, *Storm* once more gathered way through the torrential downpour. I was not quite sure where I was at the moment, and with helm again pegged I stood on the port-side deck and sounded continually. Neither shore could be seen now, and not even a light astern could penetrate the mass of falling water.

A flash of lightning rent the heavens and for a moment dazzled me. It was followed by a mighty crash of thunder that racketed across the sky and rumbled away over the sodden fields to the south. Unearthly silence once more closed down, broken only by the continuous hissing of the rain and the measured beat of the motor. Again the skies were filled with a blinding glare, and for an instant revealed the high cliff of Wrabness looming up against the sky close off the port bow. At the same moment the lead gave 2 fathoms. And in the pitchy darkness that followed, it seemed to me that the pattern of the flash, like a map of the River Amazon, still flamed across the sky. And while the resulting thunder-clap

95

gave vent to its terrific majesty, like the crack of doom, rolling distantly away into subdued rumblings, I stowed the dripping canvas and let go the anchor.

And when, three hours later, I went out on deck to look at the night before turning in, I found a still, starlit scene with the lights of Harwich twinkling over the mirror-like water in the distance.

But the glass was still falling.

.   .   .   .   .

It was very silly, and if I had not been so sleepy I should probably have tried to sit up and tell my berth what I really thought of it. It was doing its level best by being anything but level to pitch me right out of it. I rolled first one side and then the other, protesting feebly when the hard bunk-board caught me a blow on a curved area situated about amidships. Then I realized what was the matter. The yacht was almost rolling her decks under.

The halliards were beating a savage tattoo on the mast, and the wind in the rigging rose and fell in a penetrating shriek. Rearing and plunging, rolling and twisting furiously, *Storm* was like a tethered lion cub, and as she tore angrily at her anchor the chain rasped against the bobstay with sudden bursts of sound and snubbed against the stem.

But on deck—the wind! It was blowing a whole gale from a little north of west and straight down the narrow channel almost from the bridge at Cattawade. The wind was hurling itself against the young flood, picking off the tops of the waves in its impetuous grasp and thrashing them along in a scurry of white, driving spume. For a minute I stood in the well, holding on to the weather coaming, facing the blast. The gale roared in my ears and filled my nostrils with keen spray.

Wind! Is there anything so unconquerable when it is in a fury? Calm and gentle at times, it allows itself to be played with, smiling the while at the cock-sure demeanour of the man who potters about in his little sailing-dinghy enjoying the faint breeze; but how could this roaring power be the same thing? Merely a certain volume of air hurrying in to take the place of other air that has taken into its head to float heavenwards? What can man do against such a force but use his ingenuity and skill and pray for no accidents?

The Stour was a mass of white that dashed against the mud a cable's length to leeward and scattered the seaweed across its undulating surface. Overhead some gulls wheeled and cried and wheeled again, just holding their own against the blast for a time, then with a terrific swoop shooting to leeward at the speed of a train. This blow was not coming from the quarter I had expected, and instead of being nicely sheltered under the high cliff, *Storm* was wallowing in mid-channel, sailing gaily round her hook.

A sudden noise like the chatter of a machine-gun called startlingly from forward. The jib tier had carried away, and the clew of the sail was flacking to leeward, the sheets lashing wildly against the forestay. I crawled along the side-deck and awaited my opportunity to grab the sail. A sheet flicked across the back of my head and sent the pain up my arm like an electric shock. Two minutes of desperate struggle and the jib was again lashed to the bowsprit.

The motion of the boat as she sailed round in circles, over-running her anchor and bringing up with sickening

97

crashes on the chain, put breakfast out of consideration, and with the mud so close to leeward it would be foolish to remain. Besides, there is something in a wind like this that holds out a challenge . . .

The squalls came down harder than ever as I got in the chain link by link, while it rasped on the bobstay and groaned round the winch drum. At last the anchor was out and on deck. With a report that jerked up the bowsprit and bent the masthead eagerly forward so that the shrouds sang in unison, the medium jib was broken out, and I ran aft to the helm. Then the race began.

Standing at the vicious tiller it seemed to me that all the fiends of hell were tearing at that small triangle of tanned canvas set a couple of feet along the bowsprit. The sheet was bar taut and vibrated along the deck between the coaming and the first fairlead, like the E-string of a violin under the deft strokes of the player. The truck, with the rag of burgee quivering above it, was describing small circles against the sky, whilst astern, on the end of a long painter, the dinghy alternately stood up on end and bore down upon the transom over a seething, hollow crest, a smother of driven spray.

The scene all around was one of wild forces let loose. Had Nature gone mad? Could this uncontrollable force be the very same that at times flirted deliciously with the balloon jib and attempted so coquettishly to lift the heavy mainsheet clear of the bubbling water? And this wilderness of boiling waters, was this the peaceful Stour that, only the previous week-end, had appeared like a beautiful blue mirror? As far as the eye could reach, a mist of spume drove over the surface of the water, and the great mooring buoys below Erwarton Quay appeared

98

only at intervals to shake their black heads free of the spray that washed continually over them.

On we tore, forging over the spring flood as though it did not exist, straining and lurching, rolling and pouring off from each bow a curling wave that collided with others, turned over and scattered before the blast in flying fragments. In the harbour, smacks and bawleys were running up the Orwell from their exposed moorings under reefed staysails. Nothing else could be seen under way anywhere. As we passed as close as I dared over the middle of Shotley Spit, the wash broke on either side, and one roller crashed on to the after-deck and drenched me through my oilskins. For one hideous moment my heart seemed to stop as I wondered whether I had cut it too fine. But in twenty seconds we were over, and I glanced at my watch.

The five and a half miles from Wrabness had taken a fraction over an hour against a spring flood with the working jib only set.

Once in Sea Reach the wind came abeam, and I went to haul in a few inches of jib sheet. But I reckoned without the weight in this breeze. Once off the cleat, the sheet tore out of my hands, the jib blew out to an accompaniment of an artillery-like crackling, and in a few seconds strips of it were flying away to leeward.

The shore at Trimley Marshes was close under my lee and the yacht was rolling towards it at a sickening pace. Called hurriedly to work, Kelvin began its steady song, the bowsprit gradually came up towards the wind and laboriously *Storm* edged up towards the land on the Shotley side, where the Harwich smacks had brought up. With the anchor down once more, I cleared what was left of the jib and got the little spitfire jib ready to go up.

A horrible roll was coming in here, and before long I found the anchor beginning to drag, bit by bit. The wind was backing more towards the south-west, and even this place would be desperately uncomfortable while it lasted. The only reasonable place was on my own moorings at Pin Mill, and thither I wanted to sail. There was something wildly thrilling about these shrieking elements that had stirred something deep down in the owner of *Storm*, and in three minutes she was under way again with five reefs rolled in her mainsail—almost a balance reef—and storm-jib set. It was a sail of a lifetime.

Unnerving during the first few minutes when one looks anxiously at every creaking bit of gear and scaring throughout, there was joyous fascination about handling this stiff old ship through those squalls. With her lee-rail awash, rare enough occurrence with her, *Storm* rounded Collimer buoy and began a smashing 'long and short' through Butterman's Bay, while solid lumps of water slithered up the weather top-sides, curled over the rail and tore across the cabin-top in drenching spray.

Amongst the yachts at Pin Mill my heart seemed to beat in my mouth, but not once did the old ship let me down, and without undue fuss the mooring buoy was got aboard and the sails stowed gladly.

'Oh yes, Mr. Griffiths,' Harry Ward sang to me, later, in the inimitable voice that is part of Pin Mill, 'it blowed more'n a gale here to-day, and we've had the devil of a mix-up what with bo'ts gettin' foul and that. Yours was about the only moorin's that wasn't picked up by somebody's hook, and one bo't's gawn ashore across the other side, as you see. An' she had two anchors down, too.'

Rain and wind. They are good in reasonable quantities, but . . .

VII

Across the Estuary

W^E shall be afloat before long now.'
Bill's voice sounded as though it came from another world, as voices do when you are awakened from a doze. I sat up carefully—remembering the hardness of the oak deck beam just above my head—and peered uncertainly at the cabin clock. It was twenty to seven, and I must have fallen asleep over my book an hour ago.

'The water's nearly round us already,' his voice added from the well, while his cheerful face beamed at me through the half-open cabin doors and his eyes blinked good-humouredly through horn-rimmed spectacles. 'The wind's gone down a good deal since you started reading. It looks as if it might die altogether at sunset.'

I joined my friend in the well and sat, still with a great many 'sleepies' reluctant to leave my eyes, with my arm over the immovable tiller. The south-west wind, which had been blowing at gale force earlier in the day, was taking off and was now but a moderately fresh breeze. It had been the cause of our present position, and having driven us nicely aground on the tail end of the Horse Shoal, it had blown hard for a few hours and then, satisfied that it could not move us in any sense any farther, had lost interest and begun to die down.

Storm, thanks to her shallow draught and ample beam, was sitting almost upright, her slight list to starboard being felt more in the cabin than on deck. For nearly ten hours we had rested like that, immovable, quite still and perfectly contented, while the wind had howled and rain had pattered in volleys on the deck and cabin-top. We had sat in the slightly tilted cabin all the afternoon eating and reading and occasionally looking out through the port-holes to watch the antics of the only other yacht in this anchorage. She had pitched and rolled all day in the channel while we had merely vibrated with the wind in the rigging.

The previous day Bill and I had sailed *Storm* down the Medway from an anchorage under the shadow of Upnor Castle, below Chatham, past Queenborough and through the Swale to the mouth of Faversham Creek. Here, in the East Swale, just opposite the old ferry-house at Harty we had let go for the night, intending to push on across the Estuary the next day to the Blackwater, for our short holiday was nearly at an end.

But the barometer had dropped four-tenths during the night, and at nine o'clock, when it was high water next morning, there was a strong wind whipping off the crests of the little seas and making *Storm* snub and grind on her anchor chain.

'Too much wind for a passage outside to-day,' we had said. 'There'd be a devil of a sea crossing the Oaze Deep, and we might not be able to make the Colne; we might even be driven away to Harwich.'

The wind had agreed with us and burst upon the anchorage in a fury of driving rain and low scudding clouds, and an hour after high water *Storm* had begun to drag her anchor. But we did not worry, for a hundred

'THE WATER WAS CREEPING UP TO US'

yards under our lee the soft mud of Horse Shoal was uncovering like a flat pudding, the little waves breaking furiously round the windward side, leaving a rim of white froth. *Storm* took the mud gently and ceased to drag. The waves broke impotently against her black bows for a little time, growing less fierce as the tide dropped; all movement in the old boat subsided, and slowly the little waves retreated, leaving us sitting in an expanse of flat mud over which froth was blown like down before the wind, while the gulls wheeled and planed over their feeding-ground with weird devilish cries.

From where we lay we could see across the fast uncovering flats to the distant town of Whitstable. Some of the oyster smacks, which had for a few hours been riding to their moorings, pitching slowly in the swell when the tide was up, now lay still, all hope of going to sea gone, their masts at rakish angles pointing forlornly in different directions. Beyond Shellness, the most easterly point of the Isle of Sheppey, we watched through the glasses a Thames spritsail barge sailing close-hauled up towards the London River, hugging the Kentish shore as close as she dare to gain its shelter and avoid as much of the ebb as she could. She had lowered her topsail and mizen and was heeling appreciably under a slightly-brailed mainsail and foresail, the spray driving in sheets over her bluff bows.

During the afternoon a small, white motor cruiser fought her way into the East Swale from the turmoil outside, and dropped her anchor above us in the channel. There were two men and two women aboard, and they appeared thankful to have got in, for they all went ashore later in the dinghy, while the cruiser, in the manner of high-sided power craft, sheered wildly about on her anchor, rolling furiously.

'All the joy of cruising in these places,' observed the mate as he watched her, 'would go if I had to do it in a motor-boat. Think of taking *that* damn thing up a creek on a still night, disturbing the peace with the noise of that engine, and knowing that wherever you go you've got to put up with its continual racket.' He sat there fumbling savagely in a time-worn tobacco pouch. 'Just fancy having nothing to do but stand at a wheel all day and steer while the engine just shoves you along!' He bent down, shielding the match from the wind, then sat up and pulled contentedly at a crackling pipe. 'I don't mind having an engine aboard like you've got here, just to use in emergency, but more'n half the joy is handling sails and halliards and *sailing* your ship around, working tides, and cheating 'em across sands. But,' and he looked round at the expanse of mud on which we were resting, 'you *do* want a boat that'll do this sort of thing comfortably on this coast, don't you?'

I nodded, knowing what he meant, for he sails mostly on the South Coast, where there is usually plenty of water for the 6-ft. draught of his own boat.

The rising tide had crept round us now, and its edge was advancing in timid, furtive little rushes of animated froth, like ginger-beer, up the smooth slope of the mud. Like a well-trained army, it was advancing towards the middle of the shoal from all sides, and we knew it would meet and obliterate the highest mound in the middle as inevitably as the setting of the sun. The gulls knew it too, for they fought more and more savagely and scolded one another with raucous cries as their feeding-ground became more and more restricted. The subdued waves were beating against our hull now with a *plop, plop,* while little green crabs fought and chased one another in and out of the advancing water.

By the time the last stronghold of the doomed island was overwhelmed and disappeared beneath the rising tide, *Storm* had begun to show signs of awakening. The tiller moved spasmodically as the water fussed round the rudder, and after a few preliminary shudders the old boat lifted herself upright, turned her bowsprit slightly away from the wind until her anchor chain became taut, then lay gently rocking, afloat once more.

Twilight was falling and I sat in a corner of the well watching the shades darkening the distant hills beyond Sittingbourne, where tall factory chimneys still stood silhouetted against the fading light in the western sky. The breeze had fallen to a steady wind now, that came warm and soft as new milk across the Kentish fields, bringing with it a variety of scents of the land, of wet grass, of farms, and sheep and seaweed. It was a wild, soothing night-wind that blew gently through one's hair and laid a tender caress on one's face.

A light suddenly appeared in the cabin, lighting up a segment of the well seat through the open door, and a Primus in the fo'c'sle started its efficient roar. The mate stepped out into the well and threw the spent match overboard.

'I've just put some soup on to warm up for supper,' he remarked, looking round the sky. 'Shall we need the riding light here? I suppose we'll move off into deeper water before turning in?'

I nodded towards the sea beyond Shellness Point that was invisible in the darkness.

'I think this wind's going to last all night,' I said;

107

'it's always steady at night, and as it's a fair wind for us ——well, what about it?'

'O.K., Skipper, you've said it. But,' Bill suddenly looked anxious, 'we'll have a good hot meal first?'

A world without good hot meals at frequent intervals would be a purgatory for Bill, although if I tell him so he invariably says he thinks not, that if it weren't for me, if in fact he weren't always considering my health when sailing with me, he could go without meals altogether himself and just be happy and good and pure on occasional simple snacks. He merely feels that it would not be good for *me* to go without plenty of good food, and so he insists on our having meals for my sake, even when food is repugnant to him, and he would rather be thinking of higher things.

You can never do anything with a fellow who can dare to argue like that.

There was very little flood left as *Storm* slipped away from the anchorage in her old mysterious manner and headed out between Shellness Point and the Whitstable Flats. This was just what she loved to do, to appear from nowhere at an anchorage, to be lying there with the other yachts at nightfall, yet when daylight came again to be gone, vanished, no one knew where.

Storm had no proper home port. It is true, if you looked at the shapely black transom that followed the lines of her big sisters, the true bawleys, you would read 'STORM— LEIGH' thereon, but that was only because she had been built at Leigh-on-Sea on the other side of the Thames. She had not visited her birth-place, so far as I know, for quite ten years; she flew no particular yacht club's burgee at her masthead, but instead fluttered there a long scarlet streamer, like those at the head of nearly all the masts in Holland. Apart from this cosmopolitan touch there was something about this little cutter that made her blend with her wild surroundings; she was a true Essex fishing type of boat, so full of character that there was no other *yacht* around the whole coast that even resembled her. It would only be amongst the fishing fleets that you might find a family likeness.

The breeze had freshened a little after nightfall, and with her sheets eased well off and her tanned sails just visible in the darkness against the stars, *Storm* seemed as though anxious to get back to the Blackwater. While the mate steered I went forward and lay on the foredeck, gazing down at the roaring bow wave, occasionally looking up at the streamer which, dimly silhouetted against the stars, fluttered forward of the mast in a long quivering streak.

It seemed as though the whole of the Thames were rushing to meet us, and as it encountered our powerful bow it sprang up and rolled over in a never-ending turmoil of greeny phosphorescence, while drops leapt forward and lit up the untroubled water ahead with tiny splashes of light, like twinkling stars that raced to join the curling wave.

The uncanny light from the breaking water lit up the jib with a ghostly radiance, while as the old boat rolled, the green rays of the starboard sidelight, which glared unwinkingly in the lee rigging, were added to the phosphorescence of the sea.

As we left the mouth of the Swale astern not a single light could be seen. It was swallowed up in the night as though it had never existed. Even the dim riding light of the little white motor cruiser was obscured now by Shellness Point. To starboard the lights of Whitstable and Herne Bay began to open out like the rows of port-holes of a liner, while as we drew abreast of Warden Point on the north shore of Sheppey the loom of South-end, some fifteen miles away, appeared like an unnatural dawn in the sky. None of the lights along the front or on the pier could be seen, however, for they would be below the horizon.

There was a considerable swell in the deeper water beyond the Columbine Spit, and long before we began to search for the unlighted East Spaniard buoy in the darkness, *Storm* was lurching and rolling with the lumpy seas coming up astern on her port quarter. She would hurry onward in a wild rush as a swell passed beneath her, boiling and roaring against her wide shoulders and lighting up every minute detail of her rigging with its pale phosphorescence; she would pause in her headlong rush as the next sea heaped itself up astern ready to overtake her, and then press onward again, pitching and scending through the night.

Soon a row of lights in the south-west that appeared every now and then above the wave-tops told us that we had opened up Sheerness, and that we ought to be seeing the light on the East Red Sand buoy before long. Already the white flash of the Girdler light-vessel was brilliant, for it was now but three miles away while the red light of the Maplin lighthouse, far ahead on the other side of the Estuary, appeared every now and then as we were lifted on the top of a swell.

This was a night in a hundred, a soft refreshing night wherein the world and its haste and troubles seemed far away and insignificant. As I lay there and gazed up at the stars that appeared to gyrate round the cross-trees like fire-flies round a bush, I felt supremely contented

110

and thankful that, whatever the weather meted out to us in these Northern Isles may seem at times, we should occasionally have nights like this to look back upon when all else is forgotten. On a night such as this the soul of man is uplifted and he——

'Say, it's about time we had something to eat, don't you think? There's some cold sausages in the grub locker.'

I could scarcely believe my ears as the mate's soulless voice broke in upon my thoughts. His carnal desires, so brutally expressed, hurt my finer feelings, which at that moment were struggling to justify themselves. There were my beautiful reflections gone for ever, returned to the stars whence they had come, and here was I sitting on a hard deck, slowly realizing that it was chillier than I had thought, while thoughts of cold sausages—cold sausages in place of stars!—were filling my mind. All through that fool of a mate's remark.

I knew Bill too well to expect him to keep quiet if I pretended to be asleep. Once he has the desire for food fully registered in his mind there is no room for anything else. He is what I call a One Idea man. If he had only taken up a business career with the same determination he would have become a shining example of Success due to Constant Application.

I got up reluctantly and walked aft, while his beaming face, which was lit up by a shaft of soft light from the cabin door, made me feel after all that while we are on this earth we may as well try to be contented with earthly things, for, taken in the right way, they are pretty good; and if it comes to that, it really had got colder and there were worse things than cold sausages and bread and brown ale to toy with even on a night like this.

I opened what Bill referred to coarsely as the grub locker, and in a few minutes we were contentedly munching to the song of the wind in the rigging.

In all directions now the lights of buoys winked and flashed, some red, some white; while here and there the steady red or green lights between two equally steady white lights denoted the silent passage of a steamer through the night. We had left the white flash of the East Red Sand buoy astern, and the occulting red light of the Shivering Sand buoy was twinkling and disappearing a mile or more on our starboard beam. The number of steamers' lights appeared suddenly to have increased and it was impossible to look round the horizon and count them several times and get the same answer each time. They seemed to spring up from all over the place; for we were about to cross their outward-bound track.

The breeze was holding true and steady, a lovely, fair wind, and *Storm* was hurrying through the inky water at five knots or more. But the ebb-tide was also pouring out of London River, away to the north, running athwart our course and carrying us bodily with it. With parallel rulers and dividers in the cabin, I pored over the chart which was spread out on the table and worked out the simplest problem in navigation, while the little brass lamp rocked in its gimballs and the water surged past our sides with a continuous *whiss-sh*.

'The tide's running in *this* direction about—let me see, the chart says, Neaps 2¼ knots—our speed is roughly five and a half. The course to clear the tail end of the West Barrow is N.¼W. Then we ought to steer—now, where did I put that pencil?'

'Have you worked out our course for the Swin yet?'

'THIS WAS A NIGHT IN A HUNDRED'

113

Bill's voice came faintly through the closed doors. The well-lighted cosy cabin seemed a different world from the one outside, and when I came out and closed the doors behind me I had to accustom my eyes to the darkness.

'Keep her going N.W.½N.,' I said, peering into the dimly-lighted binnacle, 'that'll clear the end of the Barrow quite nicely allowing for the ebb, and we ought to be able to pick up the West Barrow before long. It has two white flashes every ten seconds.'

Crossing the Thames Estuary always demands careful navigation, for the tides sweep up and down it athwart your course at from 2 to 3½ knots, and unless you allowed for them and foresaw what they would be doing, say, three hours ahead, there is no knowing where your ship might be carried. Had we made no allowance for tide, the fast-running ebb would have carried us north and certainly led us on to the Barrow Sand if we had not grounded on the Girdler or the Knock John. This shoal-infested Estuary with its strong tides has to be treated with all the respect it deserves—especially on the ebb. Nearly all these outlying and isolated sands are so hard and unyielding that if you go aground on them in a bad sea, or if a strong wind springs up while you are waiting for the tide to float you, your little ship is almost doomed. Many a good, sound yacht, many a sturdy fishing-boat has left her bones on those sands, and few places in the world have so many wrecks of seagoing ships to their account as this dangerous corner of the North Sea.

To see the angry seas breaking on the cruel granite-like sands on a breezy day in summer is to give one only a glimpse of the horror of such a place on a winter's night, when a snow-laden gale screams down out of the frozen north and lashes the Estuary into a frenzy of black waters frothing with madness. It is no place for a ship then, but food must be brought from the Colonies, fish must be caught, freights must be delivered—and so ships pass in and out down the steamer channel, running the gauntlet of these dangers as a matter of business. . . .

The night wore on, and the old Maplin lighthouse, which stands gauntly on piles at the edge of the sands, slipped past, the wash of the seas amongst the eight steel legs coming clearly to us on the night air, while the shutter rose and fell on its powerful red light with monotonous regularity. Soon the Swin middle-light float, like a miniature lightship that has lost its crew but goes on flashing its white rays because it has not learnt how to stop, had also dropped astern, and when a suggestion of light in the eastern sky heralded the interminable approach of dawn, *Storm* was sailing slowly through the Wallet Spitway.

Bill tightened the scarf round his neck and rubbed his hands together.

'Air's nippy now, isn't it? How about some hot coffee and something to eat?' And he disappeared into the cabin without noticing my agonized expression. Did he ever think of anything else, I wondered! But the roar of the Primus in the fo'c'sle sounded cheering, for as the uncertain light began to spread over the whole of the sky in the east, and first the rigging aboard our little ship, then the individual waves, slate-coloured with deep furrows of jet blackness between them, and finally the distant shore at Colne Point became visible, the air was bitterly cold and seemed to penetrate both sweaters and even the canvas fisherman smock that I was wearing.

116

When Bill handed out a steaming mug of delicious coffee made with milk and a doorstep of bread and jam, I grabbed them without any ceremony.

Acquaintances on shore who do not go sailing sometimes exclaim rapturously, 'How perfectly *mar*-vellous to be able to watch the dawn rise at sea!' Except that I could not stand having such people aboard, I wish on occasions like this they could be here to see how much pleasure there really is in watching daybreak at sea in a small yacht. I have seen a good many, and every single one has seemed hours overdue, dull, tedious, bitingly cold, and infinitely long in making up its mind what it is going to do.

You are usually feeling either dead tired or faint from continuous seasickness, or both, and when by the time you can see clearly, and your teeth are chattering and your fingers and toes have lost all feeling, the sun appears, and almost immediately a cloud gobbles him up and you probably don't see him for the rest of the day. Meanwhile, the boat plunges on and a few icy showers of spray warn you to put on your oilskins. No, I never like the dawn at sea, especially when it follows a warm, almost tropical night as this one had been.

The wind had drawn more westerly and fallen away to a light breeze, and we were only just able to lay our course up for the entrance to the Blackwater.

A few hours later in the day we were anchored close in to the shingly beach by the little jetty on Osea Island, a few yards in fact from the 'Barnacle,' that friendly old post that was planted there, so it is said, in '75 to lean the historic yawl *Jullanar* against for scrubbing, that epoch-making yacht which was built here by Bentall, the local iron-master, and which revolutionized the hull design of yachts as the sails of the *America* twenty years before had revolutionized the cut of sails.

We anchored here because the morning had turned out fine, and as there was no point in getting *Storm* up to her moorings off Heybridge club house until high water, it was more pleasant to have a late and leisurely breakfast while at anchor in this delightful spot.

The wind fell away as the sun beat down on the still water and left a glassy calm. *Storm* rode motionless, while her reflection was scarcely broken on the mirror-like surface. The flood-tide was nearly done.

'We shall have to go up under the engine,' I said.

But a fluky air, ruffling the water, saved us for the moment, and to the rattle of the anchor chain being hauled in, *Storm* spread her brown sails and drifted up as far as the last black buoy abreast Northey Island.

'This is what I like,' said the mate contentedly. 'Do it with sails is my motto.' He pointed down the river to a white speck that was overhauling us, the sound of its motor coming clearly over the water. 'Just listen to the damned racket that motor-boat's making. Positively pollutes the whole river for miles!'

The wind fell away again as the ebb started to run, and with her sails hanging listlessly and the mainsheet drooping into the water, *Storm* began to drift back ignominiously, although within sight of her moorings.

'I'm sorry,' I said reluctantly. 'I'll have to start up Kelvin.'

'What? And add to that blighter's din?'

I opened the engine-box and began to tinker.

'Oh, but this is a very quiet engine.'

When I had swung it for several minutes, tinkered feverishly with different parts, and descended from a state of pained surprise to sweating blasphemy, Bill remarked that it certainly was a quiet engine.

'What's the matter with it?' he asked innocently.

'If I knew what the devil the matter was, do you think I'd be trying every way of getting the damn thing to go, you silly ass?"

I was reduced to addressing my friend like that. But he had a motor-bike, and only smiled sympathetically.

It was no use. Some minute thing had apparently broken inside the magneto. A tiny thing, but—there you are.

'We've drifted back a long way,' Bill remarked.

I was speechless with annoyance, and began to work off some of it on the sweep—the 12-ft. oar by means of which an energetic or desperate person can convert every ounce of exertion he can muster into a propulsion effect on the yacht of about half a knot.

It was while I was putting my energy into this invention of the devil—the 'wooden tops'l' as the sweep is called—that the white motor-boat with its noisy engine drew abreast of us.

'Why,' exclaimed Bill in disgust, 'it's that little motor cruiser that came into the Swale yesterday! Don't they look awful sitting there like wax figures?'

He was at the helm and could appreciate it. The two men and the two women stared unblinkingly at us, and then, in the loud voice one has to employ aboard a motor-boat to make oneself heard above the din of the engine, a voice that will carry for miles, one of the men said:

'There y'are, Elsie, *that's* what you 'ave to do when you 'ave a sailin' yacht. Pleasures of yachtin', that is!'

VIII

Rescue at Sea

THE wind seems to have died on us,' Bill remarked quietly. 'We're only just stemming this ebb.'

I looked at a post on the shore and saw that the scenery behind it was almost stationary. We were scarcely moving an inch over the ground, although the failing breaths of this fickle breeze were giving *Storm* steerage way through the water.

'It's an equinoctial spring ebb,' I said, 'one of the highest tides of the year, and it will be running harder still in half an hour.'

I was glad that we had managed to creep round Colne Point and at least get as far as half-way up the river towards Brightlingsea Creek before the combination of a dying breeze and the turn of the tide brought us to a standstill so far as the land was concerned. Of course, we could have turned on the engine and chugged up against the strongest ebb, but I just prefer to imagine there is no engine and to try to work my ship where I want without its mechanical assistance.

We continued to sail slowly on through the water, yet fixed, as it were, motionless over the ground, while the first of the red Channel buoys surged sluggishly from side to side a few yards away as the water poured past it and gurgled incessantly.

'It'll take us an hour or more at this rate,' Bill went on,

120

'to make Pyfleet Creek. Of course . . .' and his gaze fluttered down towards the engine-box in front of him. Then he looked guiltily away.

I hid a smile and pointed towards our proposed anchorage for the night, close to the eastern end of Mersea Island.

'More than a dozen yachts brought up there already,' I remarked. 'If there's going to be no wind to-night—and the glass has risen, Heaven knows!—what's wrong with this?'

Bill gazed towards the deserted shingle beach that led, half a mile farther down, round the point, and nodded. Provided the wind did not get up from the west in the night it would be a perfectly quiet anchorage, and I knew where we could land on the shore and go for a walk if we wanted to. He, delightful companion, shares my dislike of bringing up amongst a crowd of other yachts when there are equally good anchorages near-by where one can be undisturbed. I have never been able to understand why the majority of yachtsmen seem to go to no end of trouble to make some popular anchorage for the night just because other yachts have anchored there.

The herd instinct is very prominent in many yacht owners, and one frequently sees a cluster of yachts brought up close together in a recognized anchorage, which is not by any means ideal for the prevailing wind, while other places, where perfect shelter is to be found, are quite deserted. To me one of the chief joys of cruising on this East Coast is the number of excellent and deserted anchorages where shelter can be obtained, and where you are certain not to be disturbed by other boats anchoring close by and having banjo parties or turning on a loud-speaker. That is the sort of thing that makes cruising in the Solent so depressing—the only places where you can anchor without being rolled out of your bunk by the wash of passing liners are so crowded at week-ends that it is difficult to avoid fouling some other boat if the wind gets up during the night, while a loud-speaker or a hilarious party can be heard all over the anchorage.

Bill edged *Storm* in a little towards the shore while I took a sounding.

'Well, there's four fathoms here. That'll be two at low water. We'll let go here.'

The cable rumbled out, drew her head round and tautened with a jerk as it checked the boat and the tide swilled past the quivering links, while the mate stowed the old tanned mainsail.

The wind had gone and the tail of the red streamer hung lifeless at our masthead. A small, white cutter was throbbing her way up against the tide towards the cluster of yachts farther up. She, too, wanted to be where the others were.

It was a peaceful conclusion to what had been a hard thrash round from Pin Mill, for it had blown fresh from the west earlier in the day, and *Storm* had been bucking into a steep, vicious sea in the Wallet.

It was already dusk, and when the white cutter had passed out of earshot, nothing seemed to be stirring about the mysterious gloom of the river. Yet, something did begin to stir as I stood holding on to the forestay. The streamer was fluttering languidly to a new little breeze that was coming from the north-east—off the land.

While the mate was laying the table in the cabin and the Primus was roaring merrily in the fo'c'sle, I hung up

122

the riding light on the forestay and stood for a time in its yellow gleam as darkness imperceptibly drew a veil over the scene. The cool breeze was blowing stronger now, making the ripples lap against the old ship's black sides as the tide hurried past them.

An hour and a half later, after supper, I stood in the well and peered at the black line of the shore, beyond which the loom of Clacton was reflected in the sky. It looked so mysterious that I felt urged to go for a walk there before turning in, and put the suggestion to the mate. He was willing.

'Yes, I'd like to walk that steak down a bit,' he said breezily, but I ignored the remark.

The shore where we landed was hard, and we scrunched our way along towards the point—and the sea. It was a deserted bit of coast, this strip of sedge-bordered shingle, although two miles to the north lay Brightlingsea, with its creek crowded with yachts and oyster smacks, and some four miles round the point we would come upon Clacton and its outskirts. But a mile of sedge grass and saltings, intersected by a little creek that wound its way inland from Point Clear, the next point up the river, lay between this strip of shore and the mainland, and it would have been a wearisome trudge along the beach to the nearest dwelling.

Bill suddenly stopped and pointed out a gaunt structure that loomed up against the sky above the jagged horizon of sedge, a fantastic erection like a colliery pit-shaft.

'What on earth's that thing?' he demanded in the tones you would use if you discovered a threshing-machine in your back garden.

We went up to it and stumbled over a set of contractor's rails that led beneath a shute under which some iron tip-wagons were standing, full of sand.

'I remember now,' I said; 'there is a sand and gravel pit in these parts and this must be it. These rails lead across the saltings to a quay where the wagons tip the sand into barges. I've seen a barge's sprit up here before. They must work them up that narrow little creek from Point Clear.'

As we turned away a sudden gust of wind moaned dismally through the rickety-looking structure, rising to a shriek, and a piece of sacking above our heads began to flap like the wings of some gigantic bat. Without warning, a piece of loose iron roofing fell down with a harsh clatter.

Bill turned away.

'Let's go. This place gives me the creeps!' And we instinctively quickened our steps towards the point.

When we reached the end of the land that curved round and led along the coast to the distant loom of Clacton, we sat down on the shingle close to one of the two triangle-topped beacons that mark the lower end of the measured half-mile. The Inner Bench buoy at the mouth of the Colne was sending out its shaft of light every six seconds, while farther out into the sea we could watch the white flash of the old Knoll.

'The sea's very restless on the bar to-night.'

I nodded at my companion's remark. From out there towards the invisible bar buoy came a continuous noise, not deep enough for the roar of surf nor shrill enough for the shriek of the sea's onslaught on shingle, but a steady, incessant *commotion*, like the sound of an angry crowd heard through closed doors. Its direction was uncertain; you felt it came from out there somewhere, yet you seemed more conscious of the sound when you were not actually listening for it. It was a noise that might have been going on since the world began, yet it was only to-night, here, that we seemed to have noticed it for the first time. And still it went on.

'Like an army advancing, isn't it?' remarked Bill quietly.

'It's the tides meeting over the bar.' I hardly imagined my friend needed the explanation, but I, too, was affected by the spell of the sound in some way and wanted to give its logical explanation. 'The ebbs out of the Colne and the Blackwater and down the Rays'n all meet out there and make a terrific jobble over the shallowest part of the bar. It can be a bad place with a south-easterly gale.'

But he made no comment, and for a long time we sat there saying nothing, contentedly, as two men will, listening to the whispering tides. Bill's pipe I knew was drawing well, unless my ears deceived me. We were sheltered from the wind by the hillock of grass behind us, and, for myself, I was content to rest the back of my head in my hands and gaze out over the sea at the loom in the sky above what would be Southend.

In this game of cruising there may be great satisfaction to be gained from a fast passage from one port to another, from a successful impromptu race against another yacht going the same way, from a hard thresh to windward on a fine day or from a quiet anchorage after a dusting outside; but to me one of the greatest charms of this way of life is the solitude of the nights on this eerie coast, unequalled in any other places except perhaps the moorlands or the fens, and the romance of landing on what might easily be an uninhabited island and exploring the place in the dark, stumbling across all manner of

125

surprises. At night the little ships themselves seem to change and become living things with a soul, while every breath of wind, the sound of the sea washing on the shore, the reflection of the stars on the surface of the water, even the startling cries of the wild birds as they take to invisible flight in the darkness, have a significance that is lost when morning comes.

Far away across the saltings an owl hooted, his distant screech coming down wind to us amid the rustle of the sedge grass above our heads. For a time I was silent, turning over an idea that had occurred to me.

'Are you too tired to get under way again to-night, Bill?'

'No, I'm game. Where to?'

'Well, we want to make Burnham to-morrow to pick up my new jib. Here's a jolly fine, fair wind, it'll be low water in three hours, and we could take the young flood up the Rays'n and carry it to Burnham by dawn. It seems a good opportunity.'

Within half an hour we were back aboard *Storm*, putting up the side-lights and stowing the riding light. The sail tiers were cast off and a single reef tied in the mainsail as a precaution, for if the wind did pipe up suddenly once we were in the Rays'n Channel we should not have very much room between the Dengie Flats on the west side and the Buxey Sands on the other in which to tuck in a reef. And a reef can always be easily shaken out.

Once the anchor was broken out to the *clink*, *clink*, of the winch, *Storm* turned round, heeled slightly to the pressure of the wind in her sails, and bustled forward with a bone in her teeth. We left astern the collection of swaying riding lights of the yachts anchored off East

126

Mersea hard, and soon the tall fishery buoy, pointing its intermittent white finger at us across the restless waters, slipped by with the end of Colne Point barely visible as a dark smudge beyond it.

'Look, you can just make out the beacon we were sitting under.'

I nodded, but the steering was occupying my attention, for *Storm* seemed to be in a hurry.

The lights of Clacton began to open out like a diamond necklace and the regular flash of the Knoll buoy passed away to the east. From then on we had nothing to guide us except the little compass card floating in the lighted binnacle and the distant loom of the Southend lights, until we could pick up the light of the West Buxey buoy.

It was a night full of wind, a cold nor'-easter that drove us onward, surrounded on all sides by the hiss and wash of short breaking seas as the wind met the oncoming ebb-tide over the shoals. *Storm* lunged and tossed, rolled and shook, throwing out sheets of spray from her bows. It was too dark for us to see the Buxey beacon, and even if we had sighted the old friend we should have been too close, for you have to give it at least a quarter of a mile berth to port to find the best water up the Rays'n.

The mate swung the sounding-lead and hurriedly hauled in the dripping line.

'One and a half fathoms.' His voice was blown away into the night in a queer manner.

A little later, when I judged we had passed the beacon a mile, I suggested another sounding.

'Good Lord! There's less than a fathom here!'

It was quite all right, I told him—this was the

shallowest part. We should be in a couple of fathoms again soon.

'Well, we shall hit the sand damned hard if it shoals any more,' was all he said.

The white light of the West Buxey buoy was off the port bow now, and giving this nearly a half a mile berth, we stood up towards the invisible mouth of the Crouch.

'Have to gybe now. Stand by.'

The mainsail came over with a thud and a hiss of the sheet through the blocks, and we plunged on with the wind now on our starboard quarter. Soon the low-lying coast at Shore Ends, the mouth of 'Burnham River,' could be seen and we were once more in smooth water.

'Well,' said Bill an hour later as we furled the mainsail, surrounded by the riding lights of the anchored craft off Burnham water front, 'that's been a fast passage, and it's not often you get a fair wind into the Crouch.'

'No, and what's more, this nor'easter won't last long. The glass is dropping fast already.'

.   .   .   .   .

'My goodness, what a day! Listen to that!'

The mate grinned through the haze of tobacco smoke and held up his finger. The familiar sound of the wind outside rose to a shriek that caused the mast to vibrate in its step, while a little breaking wave hit the old boat's weather bow with a heavy *plop*.

For two days we had lain on our anchor under the lee of the south shore opposite Burnham, while the southerly wind, which had followed close on the heels of our nor'easter, had risen to a gale that brought rain with it. While we sat smoking over the disordered remains of the breakfast table, low-lying grey clouds, filled with rain as though they would burst at any moment, drove overhead and the shrieking wind stirred up the waves that the rain was trying to smoothe out.

Bill and I looked at each other and the same thought occurred to us.

'Another day weatherbound, and too rough even to go ashore in the dinghy? Why not let's see what it's like outside, just for fun?'

There was some joy to-day in washing up the breakfast crockery in a hurry and stowing everything away carefully to be ready for the rough-and-tumble we knew we should get outside the river, for we had a plan of action. After enforced inertia or a period of uncertainty, the human being takes on new life, clutches at new energy, once he has decided on a plan of action.

There was a few minutes' struggle with soaked canvas and dripping reef-points as we tied in the last reef, before we could get under way. The anchor cable required our united efforts, with the help of the winch, before we could break Old Cold Nose out of the river-bed, and when he did release his muddy grasp and Bill set the little spitfire jib, *Storm* heeled to her rail under the blast of the wind.

Away we went down a straight river whose very banks appeared but mistily through the driving rain, while we stood against the weather coaming of the well, two figures hidden in oilskins, sou'westers and sea-boots. It was good to be under way again, even in weather such as this, instead of being boxed up in the cabin nearly all day. Bill's faithful pipe appeared from beneath his dripping sou'wester, bowl downwards, for the rain and spray would have put it out.

With the wind on her starboard beam, *Storm* had the

bit between her teeth and I needed both hands on her tiller to hold her from rounding up into the weather bank. The dinghy was following on the end of a bar-taut painter with its bow in the air; a continuous wave roared away from the yacht's lee-bow and swept in a foam-flecked hollow up to a second wave that humped its crest off the lee-quarter, while fine spray was blowing like smoke into the moist gloom of the river to leeward.

Through the rain squalls the crowded anchorage, with its plunging, wind-blown yachts straining at their mooring cables as they rode to the strong ebb, appeared in a haze like a picture seen through the bottom of a glass. The wind was whipping the tops off the waves over on the lee-side of the river, and the spray was climbing the stone wall and blowing over the sedge-covered top in driving sheets like steam. Fearful of the consequences if we allowed the boat to get down to leeward and then some part of her gear carried away, we hugged the south bank and drove down the river in smooth water.

'I'd say it's blowing a full gale, wouldn't you?'

Bill had to shout to make himself heard. 'Look at it out there!'

We were nearly at Shore Ends now, and as far as could be seen the sea that stretched before us appeared covered with white crests blurred by the soaking rain. The visibility in weather such as this was limited to not more than a mile, and we could not yet see the West Buxey buoy which marked the end of the sand that divided the outflowing river into the Raysand and Whittaker channels. Over to starboard the Foulness Sand was uncovering and began to stretch out from the end of the sea-wall on Foulness Island like a thin, yellow ribbon. Where it disappeared into the welter of water or rain, one could

130

not tell which, my eye caught sight of something straight and sharp that broke the even horizon.

'There's a yacht aground on Foulness,' I shouted to the mate.

He looked at the forlorn object for some time through binoculars.

'Well, she's sitting bolt upright. Must be a barge-yacht got caught trying to cross the sands just after high water, I expect. Shall we go and see if they need assistance?'

I thought for a moment.

'No. They can't come to any harm. She *is* a little barge—I can see her plainly now—and she'll float off to-night in 18 inches of water before there's any sea running. *Storm's* making good weather of this. We'll make it a fair wind and go to West Mersea.'

Although we were under the lee of the fast uncovering sands, there was a short, lumpy swell out here, and the old boat plunged and tossed grandly over the seas as we bore up and ran before the wind in the direction of the West Buxey buoy. We were more than ever glad that we had close-reefed the mainsail, for the squalls were violent, and even now *Storm* was carrying as much canvas as we should care to have had aloft on a day like this.

For a time we could see nothing. The lowlands of the Crouch, with their dykes and solitary trees, had disappeared into the gloom astern and there was nothing but the heavy, tumbling seas around us and the eternal screaming wind and driving rain. It was both raining and blowing, if anything harder than ever now, and already a halting but determined trickle of cold moisture was feeling its way down my neck. From time to time I peered under the mainsail, expecting the Buxey buoy to appear through

131

the starboard rigging at any moment. We must pick it up, for we could not see more than half a mile now, and if we passed it without seeing it we should be on the sands themselves—a deadly lee-shore with the tide falling.

'Look, there it is!'

To my astonishment Bill was pointing over the port bow. Every now and then it appeared as it lifted on a crest, a shapeless black object almost smothered in spray. I altered our course and pointed the bowsprit at it.

'Tide must have taken us more easterly than I reckoned,' I said, not without annoyance, for we might easily have missed it altogether.

'But—hang it!—that's not the Buxey buoy.'

My companion was looking through the glasses.

'Why, it's a *boat*!' He was excited now. 'And there's someone in it waving something!'

His words gave me a thrill and I clutched at the binoculars, trying to hold them in one hand while continuing to steer with the other. Sure enough it *was* a boat. It had been end on when we had first sighted it, and now, as it suddenly appeared on the back of a wave, it had swung round and lay broadside on—a large dinghy or motor-boat—and an oar with something white on the end was being waved back and forth.

'For Heaven's sake don't gybe her!'

Bill's voice just saved a gybe all-standing, and I handed him back the glasses.

'We'll have to pick 'em up, Skipper.' His eyes were dancing with excitement now behind his spectacles. 'They're probably a fishing-party with a broken-down engine.'

'But it's all shoal water here,' and I waved my hand

132

at the high-breaking crests all round us. 'We've missed the Buxey buoy and I reckon we're out of the Rays'n. Take a sounding, Bill.'

'There's a fathom and a half here.'

'That's about 6 ft. in the hollows.' We were less than half a mile from the boat now. 'My God, if we *did* hit the sands with a sea like this running——'

'Fathom and a quarter. I say, it's shoaling, Maurice——'

'Then that boat's somewhere over the sands, either the Buxey or the Dengie Flats.' I felt desperate. 'If they're drifting over the Buxey with the ebb and wind taking them, Heaven help us, but if they're on the *west* side of the channel, there's a hope. We might be able to get to them.'

Bill pointed to our dinghy.

'D'you think I could row over while you hove-to and——'

'God, no! It'd never carry two in this sea. No, hang it, we'll risk it. That boat already looks half waterlogged, and they haven't a hope with this wind and tide carrying 'em away from the coast.'

One more sounding gave us one and a quarter fathoms. With *Storm's* 3¼-ft. draught she might still be able to float clear of the deadly sand. I blessed the old boat's shallow draught that day.

Lest we should get any more shocks I told Bill to put the lead-line away.

'Have a line ready to throw them.'

The boat was less than half a cable's length away from us now, and I brought *Storm* round a little so as to place her close to windward of the helpless craft, while Bill stood by coiling a rope ready to throw. The seas were meeting our weather bow with great crashes that

133

sent a shock through the whole ship and smothered us in heavy spray.

'Back your jib, Bill, we'll heave-to to wind'ard of him and give him a lee.'

As *Storm* rounded up close to windward of the boat we were surprised to find it a yacht's dinghy with an outboard motor on the transom and two young fellows, little more than boys, in it. What appeared so unusual was that both of them were garbed solely in underwear! They looked like a none too complimentary advertisement for Jaeger on a wet day. Their dinghy was already half awash, and the seas, all of which were tumbling over with a continual roar, were dashing more and more water into it every few seconds.

One of the boys caught our line and made it fast, while the other, who had been bailing all the while, dropped the bailer and collapsed over the midship thwart.

At that moment a bigger sea than ever caught the dinghy and carried it bodily to leeward, the line tautened as *Storm* plunged into the succeeding hollow, and parted with a vicious thud. A howl of anguish reached us from the boat as it was carried with its two wretched occupants farther astern.

'Let draw your jib.' I had the helm hard up by now. 'We'll have to gybe her. That boat can't keep afloat much longer.' Then, as *Storm* gathered way once more, I turned to the drifting boat and cupped my hands. 'We've got to gybe. We won't leave you, but keep bailing, you —— fools! And let your painter go with an oar for a sea-anchor!'

Our entire attention was taken during the next few minutes in handling *Storm*. For gybing in such a wind

134

and sea was a ticklish operation that I would never have risked in any other circumstances. The seas were dangerously steep, for we were in shoal water—exactly how much I dared not think—and one wave broke on to our after-deck, half filling the well with a boiling torrent of sand-filled water, as the mainsail slammed over with a heavy crash.

The boat with the two fellows in it was still afloat, but lifting sluggishly to the ever-increasing seas, and only appearing as it rose to a crest. One of the boys was bailing, but the other was still lying across the thwart as though unconscious. Once more I tried to manœuvre *Storm* just to windward of them so as to give them a lee, but again a sea caught hold of the boat and swept it away like a sodden box, and a howl of dismay followed us as we paid off for another gybe.

'We'll stand by you! Keep bailing!' It was all we could shout to them.

To handle a small yacht at all in a sea like this was difficult enough, but to place her exactly, with all way stopped, a few yards to windward of a drifting boat, which could only be seen now and then, needed a great deal of practice, and four times more did we make the attempt, only to find *Storm* stopped by a sea some yards short, or the boat carried away from us. Meanwhile, both vessels were being carried farther out away from the shelter of the invisible coast by the ebb-tide and the gale, and the seas were rapidly gaining in size and viciousness. It was clear that only a matter of minutes would elapse before the half-waterlogged dinghy would fill and sink. And any moment our keel might touch the sand with a sickening crash that may start a plank or even bring our mast down . . .

'Listen, Bill. Get the kedge warp and throw 'em that as I sail her slowly past the boat, and ease it round a cleat when the strain comes. It's our only chance, for they won't last another five minutes.'

The active occupant of the boat caught the heavy rope this time and managed to make it fast, and as it tautened Bill tried to ease it round a cleat. But the warp took charge, tore itself out of his hands and began to smoke through the fairlead. By good fortune a turn, or kink, in it caught, and my companion deftly made it fast.

As the dinghy gathered way in tow of us, one of the boys tried to pull it up to the yacht, and for a moment its bows dived.

'Get aft, you something idiot,' I roared, 'and keep aft! We've got to tow you into deeper water!'

Through the rain and spray, as we plunged out towards where we hoped the deeper water was to be found, the familiar Buxey beacon loomed up like an immense cross-roads sign-post. The usual cormorant was not there to-day.

'Thank God,' breathed the mate fervently, 'now we know where we are.'

Here we hove-to and hauled the boat alongside. With the help of the older boy, whose teeth were chatting with the cold, we dragged the limp figure of the other over the rail, and while I veered their dinghy astern on the entire length of the warp so as to clear our own dinghy, Bill took the two below, where they were relieved of their soaked undergarments and rolled up in blankets in the two bunks. Then he, stout fellow, managed to light the Primus in the fo'c'sle, and, in spite of the wild antics of the yacht as I got way on her again, made hot Bovril for the two unfortunates.

THE AUTHOR

It was not until we were racing up towards Mersea Quarters with our lee-rail nearly awash and both dinghies dragging along astern in a welter of spray that he reappeared, wiping his glasses, and I heard the story.

'They're both asleep now.' He looked round at the wild scene, his gaze coming to rest on their dinghy, towing just above water far astern. 'What a blessing we happened to come this way. I'll bet there's nothing else under way to-day, bar steamers.' He bent down into a corner of the well and managed to get his pipe alight. 'That barge-yacht we saw on Foulness belongs to them. She's the *Wavecrest*, of Leigh. They ran aground early this morning coming across to find shelter from the Thames. They got the anchor out, apparently, and then the dinghy parted its painter and went drifting away. The elder chap—he says he's 17—threw off his clothes, dived in and got aboard, and then found he couldn't pull the heavy boat back against wind and tide.'

'But what about the outboard engine on the stern?'

'Oh, that. As luck would have it they'd unscrewed the plug and kept it in the yacht's cabin to keep dry! Well, the youngster—he's two years younger than the other —slipped off *his* clothes and swam out and joined his pal, and there they both were in the dinghy, pulling like blazes back to their yacht, which was hard on the sands. Then they broke an oar and the wind and tide did the rest, so that it wasn't long before they lost sight of *Wavecrest* and drifted out into oblivion. They must have been adrift for over four hours before we hove in sight.'

Two days later our rescued mariners, with admirable spirit, had salvaged their small barge and continued their holiday cruise none the worse, apparently, for their narrow escape, while Bill and I found ourselves 'heroes' in the local papers which carried the story of the 'Yachtsmen's Gallant Rescue in Heavy Sea' and so on. It was a wonderful story—as it appeared in the Press!

IX

'Wintry Weather Continuing'

IT was a murky-looking evening, black, still, and
oppressive, with a very fine drizzle gently falling.
As I rowed the dinghy down the creek the lights of
the yacht club house astern looked cheerful and
almost inviting. The festive decorations could still be
seen through the windows, and a babel of shrill voices
came from within, mingled with the kind of laughter
men make when they wish to goodness the ladies would
go home and leave them to yarn amongst themselves.

Both my shipmate and I were anxious to get aboard
the old hooker, light the stove and start airing our
bedding and blankets. It was three weeks since we had
been aboard, and in December things soon become
damp in a boat. The rhythmic splash of paddles and the
rattle of loose rowlocks sounded towards us, and presently
a long, low shape was slipping by a few feet away.

'Good-night,' called a gruff voice; 'An' a merry Christmas!'

We returned the ancient greeting, and the duck-punt
with its solitary occupant vanished into the gloom astern.

It was so dark the banks of the little creek were scarcely
visible. I rested on my oars and let the overloaded
dinghy drift down on the ebb, listening for the sounds
of the night. Duck were talking loudly from the direction
of the Wades and the mud was hissing on either side as

141

the water left it like the sound of clapping coming faintly over the wireless. No other sound broke the stillness of the night, for the club house was out of earshot by now.

'Pull away, old man, it's getting horribly cold out here!'

I gazed at the pale blob in the darkness which was the shipmate's face and wondered how on earth she could feel cold with three jerseys, a reefer jacket, thick trousers stuffed into fisherman semi-thigh boots and topped by a muffler, an oilskin, and a wool cap! But, of course, I had been rowing.

Presently a big, white shape loomed up and we clutched at the side of old *Afrin*. Her rail was clammy and cold and her decks were slippery. Her cabin smelled chill and damp when I lit the lamps, but while my shipmate transferred the prodigious load of 'Christmas eats' from the dinghy to their respective lockers, I fiddled lovingly with my special joy aboard—the coal stove. Soon there was a welcome roaring and a cheerful light flickered in the fo'c'sle. Soon, too, the thermometer in the saloon evinced ambition and rose from forty steadily towards its normal sixty-eight. Round the stove in the fo'c'sle we stacked the cabin-berth cushions and blankets and opened all the lockers so that the warm air could circulate throughout the ship. Surely this is better for a boat than to be laid up in a clammy mud-berth, sweating for five months throughout the winter until the spring sun drives the mould and damp away?

While the shipmate was busily cooking dinner and a delicious smell of roast potatoes and chicken and soup came from the fo'c'sle, I went on deck to look at the night. The fine rain had stopped and the sky was clearing in parts, for stars were twinkling here and there. A faint

142

breeze had sprung up from the south-east and the halliards were beginning to brush gently against the mast. My eyes grew accustomed to the starlit darkness, and I found I could just make out the low bank on either side. The only lights visible were those of the yacht club house half a mile up the creek, with the lights of Walton behind them; while in the opposite direction a broken line of twinkling lights showed where Dover-court and Harwich lay. There was a glare in the sky above Felixstowe, but only by standing on the cabin-top could I discern the lights of the town.

The little breeze was ruffling the water now, and *Peanut*, our dinghy, began to chuckle over a secret joke. The sparks and smoke that poured out of the little chimney in the foredeck were drifting away into the darkness to leeward. I paced up and down the side-deck in contentment. Dear old *Afrin*, she was a real ship to have beneath one, small though she was. Thirty-four feet from her stem to the end of her blunt counter, 30 feet on the water-line, 10-ft. beam, only 4½-ft. draught, full-bodied, heavy, sturdy, and about to celebrate her forty-fourth Christmas. Originally a little pilot-cutter at Lowestoft, and now . . . well, she had been our honeymoon ship and our only home until the end of October, until the cold dark mornings and the weariness of the 70-mile train journey to London and back each day had driven me to take a flat in Hampstead for the winter.

Stars now showed almost all over the sky, and the light breeze had settled definitely in the east-sou'-east. I joined the warmth and light below with a suggestion.

'Why not get under way after dinner and take the first of the flood into the Stour?'

143

I have never known my shipmate give a negative reply to that sort of question.

An hour later *Afrin's* heavy mainsail went up, and with her jib and staysail drawing she rustled down the lonely creek, while the smoke from the chimney floated past the ray of light from the cabin port-holes like an endless procession of phantom forms. The faint light from the stars just enabled us to make out Stone Point and the black buoys on the edge of the Pye Sands. It was just slack water and the wind was very light, veering slightly more easterly. It compelled us to make three or four boards to clear the Crab Knoll, but from thence we were able to lay our course to the lights of Felixstowe Dock, which would clear the end of Dovercourt break-water. Soon the Pye End buoy slipped past into the night and nodded solemnly at us. He knew we should be the only yacht he was likely to see this Christmas. Poor, lonely thing.

The breeze freshened slightly, and *Afrin*, with freed sheets, hurried up the harbour, the wave from her lee-bow turning over into foam that was lurid from the glare of the port sidelight. What a wonderful night, so close to Christmas! I sat without a coat on the foredeck, which was dry from the warmth below, and when my hands got cold I warmed them round the chimney. We slipped past an anchored barge, silent and eerie in the rays from her riding light. The red occulting light of the Guard buoy came closer and its sonorous bell gave us one mournful clang, as we slipped by on the flood.

'Mainsheet!'

I walked aft at the shipmate's reminder and ran out the mainsheet as we pointed up the Stour, the breeze dead aft. The lights on Harwich Quay, with here and there a red and green one, slipped by. Next the bright glare where the train-ferry lay in her dock swallowing Anglo-Belge railway trucks. Then past the even brighter glare of the arc lamps above Parkstone Quay, with the noise of the three night steamers awaiting their train-loads of passengers from London and the North. After that—blackness.

The Stour stretched before us invisible, shrouded in darkness, unpierced by a single light. We seemed to be sailing into a world of gloom and eternal night. But we had our own little world with us, and when I went below to attend to the stove I found it throwing a cheerful red glow on to the side of the fo'c'sle and the cabin thermometer up to the seventies. So we felt our way by guesswork and lead up to our old anchorage under the cliff at Wrabness. Even as the old hooker snubbed on her chain and the shipmate began to stow the obstinate mainsail, our little breeze died away and left us floating motionless in a wonderful calm.

So utterly still was it that we stepped into the dinghy in order to drift silently past the old ship on the tide and gaze upon her unbroken reflection in the glassy water. The smoke from the chimney rose in spirals as vertical as the mast until it passed out of the rays of the riding light, and the faint soughing of the trees on the dark cliff above us had given place to an unearthly stillness. Then the sound of a train grew into a roar and clatter as it passed in the cutting behind the silent fields, and faded away into distant thunder as its lights appeared, like a luminous caterpillar, a few minutes later, to sweep round the curve and merge into the twinkling lights of Parkstone Station five miles away.

145

'That's the first of the boat-trains from Liverpool Street,' I said, and the unheeded remark sounded empty as it echoed mysteriously from the beach.

Then we clambered once more aboard and peeled off sweaters and sea-boots, for it was approaching a tropical temperature in the cabin.

'The glass is extraordinarily high,' I said, as I tapped it, 'and still rising.'

'Wind. From the east.' The ship's meteorological expert spoke with a tone of finality.

'But it's a bally flat calm!'

She pulled the day's weather map, which the Meteorological Office send her every morning, out of her locker and spread it out on the swing table.

'There's an area of unusually high pressure centred *here*, and it's moved *that much* since yesterday. If we don't get a pretty fresh easterly wind to-morrow——'

'——You'll become a nun, movie star, or police woman, and give up yachting and me. Well, we're all ready to clear out if need be.'

But the calm still held when I banked up the little stove for the night and put the damper on its chimney.

.   .   .   .   .

The weather prediction had been correct. There was half a gale blowing from the nor'-east in the morning, and when I went on deck from the warm cabin—for the stove was still merrily alight and only needed raking and recharging—the bitter cold seemed to pierce both jerseys like muslin. *Afrin* was lying to the flood, her bowsprit rising and falling as the white-crested seas passed under it. The sky was leaden, and the deserted Stour looked bleak and cold as far as the eye could

146

reach. Could this wintry scene be the same spot that had been so fairy-like but twelve hours before?

During breakfast the wind increased and moaned more shrilly in the rigging. This was an exposed anchorage, and as soon as the ebb set in it would become an intolerable berth. But our idea of cruising at Christmas was to *sail* from place to place, not lie in a 'snug anchorage' all the time.

While we were getting two reefs down in the mainsail, tugging at half-frozen reef-points with hands that had lost their feeling, a violent snow-laden squall screamed down on us, the powdery flakes driving into our ears and up our sleeves, and settling in little white drifts against the forehatch, the cabin-top and the mast. We left the mainsail half-reefed and went below to thaw in front of the stove and drink a mug of hot coffee.

My wife looked out through the skylight at the driving snow-storm.

'I believe we're dragging!'

Yes, we were. Only a little, but each time *Afrin's* powerful bow rose and snubbed on her chain, she drifted a few feet farther inshore.

'Third reef, Pete, and storm jib. We'd better hurry.'

The shipmate was on deck in five seconds. The snow was ceasing, but the wind still blew strongly, and the sky looked just as hopeless and leaden to windward. Getting the anchor was a long and heavy job, and the winch needed all my strength as the cable came in inch by inch. As soon as *Afrin* was under way and the hook catted 'Brittlesea fashion,' we hove-to for a few minutes' spell of rest. Then close-hauled on the port tack we headed down the Stour, butting into the steep little seas and throwing the cold spray across the foredeck. For

147

minutes at a time the old hooker sailed herself while we sat on the engine-box under the lee of the cabin-top which extends partly over the well. The snow had gone now and the wind seemed to be taking off. The ebb had set in and there was more than a suggestion of a break in the sky.

On either side the wild banks of the river showed in strong contrasts of black and white, where trees rustled leafless branches amid snow-covered fields. Yet somehow there was a queer fascination about the scene, even under these wintry conditions, and when quite suddenly the wind died away to a faint little breeze and the pale sun burst through the clouds, the beauty of the river and the joyousness of this care-free, elemental life made us sing and shout all the songs we knew. The shipmate showed her energy by shaking out the third reef and resetting the heavy, snow-encrusted mainsail with two reefs only. Then she went below to warm her benumbed hands and to hand up a steaming mug of Bovril. While the sunshine lasted it seemed as though it would be one of those rare days in winter, when it is almost warm and a balmy breeze blows, like a miniature trade-wind. But it was not for long. The sky became overcast once more, and when we started a long and short beat up Sea Reach in the Orwell, another snow-storm burst upon us from out of the nor'-east, as savage and bitter as the first.

Hove-to, *Afrin* looked after herself, as boats of her type will, hardly heeling at all, while we went below and stoked up the stove. What a treasure that little bogie stove was, and how we blessed it this Christmas! When the squall passed we had a tough peg to get round Collimer buoy against the strong ebb, but once round we eased the sheets and with wind abaft the beam stormed up towards Pin Mill with the snow-flakes settling everywhere about us.

I have a vivid recollection of the shipmate standing on the slanting weather deck like a young smacksman, her red thigh-boots wide apart, a muffler and blue-stocking cap almost meeting at her nose, her right hand thrust into her jacket pocket, the other holding the tiller line, the snow driving past in a continuous white storm, while the wake gurgled and hissed in the lee-scuppers.

'She's going like a train, sonny! Isn't this great!'

We took ten-minute spells each at the helm.

Pin Mill looked as deserted as the Stour. One or two yachts were laid up in the saltings with snow-covered tarpaulins over them, and only two yachts—an old 6-ton cutter and a Bristol Channel pilot-boat—lay at moorings, deserted, shabby, and forlorn. We let go and struggled with canvas as stiff as cardboard.

Not until long after dark did we again appear on deck. It was Christmas Day, and I defy anyone to want to leave a cosy cabin at a steady temperature of seventy degrees after such a Christmas dinner as we had prepared and dealt with in the orthodox manner, in order to face a blizzard on deck!

So Christmas Day was spent in warmth and comfort after some invigorating sailing, and when we left the old yacht there the next day because her anchor had dragged and fouled a mooring that had beaten even our winch, while a heavy gale from the north shrieked down upon us, snow laden and piercing, we came to learn that the poor folks ashore had had a bad Christmas. The railways had lines blocked, villages were isolated,

149

friends' cars were buried in snow-drifts, thousands of people were snow-bound away from their homes, the entire countryside was held up.

'I think,' said the shipmate with a twinkle, 'we'd better *sail* home.'

X

'Enough to Try a Saint'

FOR three weeks the south-west wind had been unceasing. Day after day with such monotony that one felt the Meteorological Office must be on holiday.

And within the limits of a fortnight's holiday we were hoping to work down West. Hopefully I had bought charts of the Lizard and the Scillies, the Channel Islands, even Ushant and Belle Isle, for I felt they ought to be aboard—in case.

'If we get a good leading wind,' I had said weeks before, 'we'll slip through the Downs and run down the middle of the Channel and make Cherbourg our first port of call.'

But when the first day of my release from an office chair came, and *Wilful* slipped down the creek, it was a run out to the Pye End buoy, off Harwich Harbour, and then a dead nose-ender to the Naze.

'There's no indication of a change,' was my gloomy opinion. 'We'll just have to plug down Channel as far as we can. So, instead of standing out to the Long Sand Head and beating all the way up to the Foreland, we'll just beat round to the Colne, have a few hours' rest, and then be able to make a fetch of this south-west wind through most of the swatchways to the Edinburgh. That'll save us a long beat.'

Which, if you look at a chart of the Thames Estuary, is sound logic. Thus the first night was spent at anchor off Pyefleet Creek opposite Brightlingsea, and next morning—it is difficult to write this—the south-west wind had gone and a light south-east breeze was in its place! Thus we had our beat after all, out past Colne Point, down the Wallet again and through the Wallet Spitway and across the Middle Deep, short boards against a fickle head wind. But once in the Barrow Deep it allowed us to run sedately against the ebb with the big, white spinnaker set, for the breeze was drawing into the east.

I clapped the mate on the back.

'Isn't it great, old thing? An easterly wind down Channel after all!'

'We're not off the South Foreland yet,' was all she said, and I clambered down the companion, feeling damped.

Dusk was falling over a peculiarly grey and misty Estuary as we took in the spinnaker, gybed and set our course over the swatchway between the S.W. Sunk and the Knock John, which would lead us into the Edinburgh. It was nearly low water, but according to the chart the least depth anywhere through this swatch-way was $2\frac{1}{4}$ fathoms.

Suddenly we hit the bottom with that dreadful jarring thud that shakes all the rigging—lifted in the slight swell, glided noiselessly forward, descended gracefully, and —thud! Again and again. The gear was rattling and shaking and an odd cup in the pantry was clinking madly. Thud, thud! It was like hitting granite, and the jarring was so bad that it was difficult to keep our feet.

Hurriedly I jumped into the dinghy and sounded around, to windward, forward, to leeward, everywhere.

It was all flat—flat as a dish with only 5 ft. between the swells. Bewildered and uncertain of the next step, I clambered aboard the complaining *Wilful* and examined the chart, took cross-bearings of the Mid-Barrow light, the Barrow No. 8 light buoy, the No. 3 red occulting buoy in the Black Deep and even the TH No. 1 green and white buoy, at the end of the swatchway.

There was no doubt about it; we were right in the middle of the swatchway, just where the chart said '2¼ fathoms.' And *Wilful*, with her 5 ft. 6 in. draught, was lifting and dropping on pavement-like sand, threatening to relieve herself of her 4½-ton lead keel.

And still it went on. As darkness fell the wind increased a little. The sheets were flattened in and the motor started and run slowly, and gradually she bumped and thudded her way, foot by foot, across the treacherous, unforgiving sand. The wind eased off, shifted a point farther north, then blew up fresh again with a dash of cold rain. *Wilful* lay farther over, bumped twice more, then gathered way for the friendly light of the Edinburgh like a hare.

The wind was in the nor'-east now, cold, with a hint at rain, and as we tore through the Edinburgh Channel with a roaring wave under our lee-bow, the dark white-crested seas rolled up abeam, lifted us, tussled with our wash and slid to leeward, their backs streaked with foam.

'This is *sailing*!' The anxiety of the sands over, I was exultant. 'Now for a run down Channel!'

When we had passed the Tongue the wind increased still more and brought a heavy driving rain with it that made the distant North Foreland light look dim. It seemed to take a prodigious time to pass the North-East Spit, and a still longer time to bring the rain-blurred North Foreland abeam.

It was a black night, black as pitch, for the jib was not visible from the little self-draining well, and the wind had gradually worked its way into the north-north-east. The ebb set in as we brought the Elbow buoy abeam about midnight, and high, white-capped seas piled up astern and came roaring at us from out the blinding darkness.

Once the dinghy swept up and hit the transom with a crash that would have put the rudder out of action had it been hit.

'Where's the stern drag painter?' yelled the mate from under her sou'wester.

My heart sank.

'Coiled up neatly on the floor of the dinghy.'

When we go to sea, my wife and I, with a dinghy in tow, we always (Always? Well, nearly always) bring a long painter aboard from the stern of the dinghy, which is kept slack until it is required to be cast overboard to steady the little boat. On this occasion I had forgotten, and left the drag painter in the bottom of the dinghy.

There was nothing for it but to heave-to and get the wretched thing overboard, for the dinghy was becoming unmanageable and would soon part its main painter. As *Wilful* swept round and put her weather bow into the trough of the next sea, the crest crashed aboard and flooded the deck. But there were no openings, for the main hatch amidships was shut, and I had remembered to replace the cowl ventilator abaft the mast with a screw deadlight.

It was while we were hove-to that we realized how hard it was blowing, and how big the seas had become. *Wilful* was rearing and pitching like a true broncho.

154

While the mate held an electric torch, I lay on the side-deck and hauled in the dinghy. The precious painter had got washed under the after-thwart in a nice tangle! A boathook at last freed it, and in a few minutes it was trailing astern. Then I eased the dinghy off on its 10-fathom bass painter until it was swallowed up in the night, and although we ran on through some of the biggest and steepest breaking seas I have ever seen, the dinghy gave no further trouble.

But the night was troubling us. The rain came down more heavily still, and the Gull light was damped out. Steering by the oil-lighted binnacle before a strong wind and a steep sea slightly on the quarter, with no reef in and obviously too much canvas aloft, was a nightmare, with the only blessing that there were no unlighted buoys ahead and that the boat steered like a lamb.

Once three great seas, larger than all the others, roared up under our weather quarter, smothered the deck in foam and actually carried *Wilful* bodily to lee-ward as she nearly broached-to with a sickening movement that was like leaping off a cliff. For one unforgettable instant I imagined we must be in shoal water —the sensation of our keel hitting the hard Knock John was still in my mind—but we rushed on with our hearts thumping, into the blustering, rain-swept blackness, with the Gull light now just visible.

What a run that was! A wild night in all truth, the roaring angry seas with their death-like blackness capped by a seething ghostly whiteness, the drenching, beating rain and the utter darkness that blotted out even our masthead. The mate, a dim figure in oilskins and sou'wester, was standing her two-hour trick with one

155

arm on the tiller, silent, and probably as apprehensive as the Skipper.

'We *must* get some canvas off her!' I shouted at last, staring blankly up at a mass of sail I could only just see.

Her hand touched my arm.

'No, don't. You might—go overboard—my God, if you did——'

And when I faced the weather astern and watched, appalled, the crests coming down on us, each one by some miracle to disappear under the able quarters, I had to admit the wisdom of her remark. But something had to be done, for *Wilful* was running like a scalded cat and beginning to yaw. We had so obviously run too long.

A few memorable minutes followed while I crawled along the deck on all fours, at one terrible moment being rolled involuntarily against the life-lines. If there had been only a foot-rail . . . The falls of the main and peak halliards were in a sodden tangle, but in due course five rolls were turned in the mainsail with the worm-gear, and I crawled aft again, breathless but as relieved as the little ship herself. I blessed the Woodnutt's gear that night, whatever else I may have thought of roller gears.

Once, a steamer's lights suddenly appeared ahead, end on. We sheered hurriedly to port and a great bulk lumbered by close off the boom end. When the thump of her propeller passed I began to breathe again. They would probably not have seen our side-lights in that driving rain and spray. After that we kept a very careful look-out into the murk ahead. The rain began to ease off by degrees, and we could now see the continuous flash of the South Foreland light over the bowsprit end. But it looked far away, dim and yellow, as though it did not belong to this world at all. The wind began to take off rapidly, and within an hour of dawn it suddenly fell away altogether, leaving us jumping and slamming in a fearsome swell, while the mainsheet block screamed back and forth over the iron horse.

In the first glimmer of the coming day we passed close to the Gull light-vessel, with a little breeze that had sprung up from the north-west. The light on the Gull became paler as the dawn spread over the sky and the mournful bleat of the fog-horn seemed in keeping with the dreary waste that lay all around us. It was cold, bitterly cold, and while the mate lay asleep in her bunk, I lashed the tiller and lit the fire in the saloon.

And so Deal, dreary and deserted at this early hour, passed by and the day was born. Oh, the blessedness of that little fireplace, with the warm shelves at the back, where our clothes could dry! And this was July. But never mind, we were opening out Dover piers, and with this nor'-westerly wind off the land we should be able to fetch all the way down Channel with smooth water and —even as we opened the Channel the wind backed to west, hesitated, and then flew into the south-west. *Wilful* headed more and more off shore and soon we had Dover piers on our quarter. Down Channel the scene was just as I always seem to have known it—a grey tumbling waste of water and a cruel wind that blows up in one's teeth.

The mate appeared sleepily through the main hatch and looked across at the white cliffs and stoneworks of the harbour. The sun was just over the horizon.

'Shall we go in?'

I knew she'd hate to, and anyway, we weren't really tired—yet.

157

'No. We'll plug on.'

And we did. The sun strengthened as the south-west wind freshened and the cliffs of Cap Gris Nez showed clearly above the restless horizon, a sure sign of wind. I staggered down the companion into the saloon and looked at the barometer. It was low, and it had dropped another tenth. But what did that matter? *Wilful* could see any gale out and, in any case, we could at least run back if it began a real blow, while if you ever go into Dover Harbour with a south-west wind you never leave, for the sight of the white horses rolling past outside is sufficient to demoralize anyone.

From now onward we kept our regular sea-watches —four hours on, four off, with the dog-watches in the afternoon. I have come to the conclusion it is not a good arrangement, the watches below being too short and the result too exhausting. But I was totally unable to get any sleep, try as I might, and spent a miserable watch below, trying to get food that I could scarcely swallow or induce sleep in a berth that seemed to have gone mad. Hours ceased to be; I could scarce remember whether it was morning or afternoon during my last watch, simply whether it was light or dark.

Only 30 ft. over all, with a length of 28 ft. 6 in. on the water-line and 8 ft. 6 in. beam. *Wilful* was making a brave fight against the big seas rolling up Channel. She was a magnificent boat for her size, a true thorough-bred, and one of the best Sibbick designed. Built at Cowes in 1899, she was flush decked with a small self-draining well right aft.

But with her lead keel so low down her movements were so bad that one was rolled about helplessly, however much one tried to get wedged in the berth. The terrific

158

descents into the troughs of the seas, the sudden impacts
on the weather bow that jarred the ship and sent water
gurgling over the deck overhead and the violent lurches
all made sleep and any form of rest, for me, impossible.
But the mate, who can sleep at any time and anywhere,
was able to tumble into her bunk at the end of her trick
on deck, removing only oilskins and thigh-boots, and
sleep like a log until called. How I envied her!

So we thrashed on, standing out towards the French
coast, coming about at the change of the watch, exchang-
ing half a dozen words, then standing in again to the
Sussex cliffs for another watch, to find, maybe, that we
had progressed six miles in that time! Some watches,
when the ebb ran, but the seas were bigger, we made
good way and got well to windward of a three-masted
tops'l schooner that came across from the French coast.
But the sun shone part of the time and it would have been
glorious to have been in the mood to appreciate the
beautiful translucent green of the water and the mag-
nificence of the long rolling seas that we climbed up and
slid over, after the short muddy seas of the Thames
Estuary, if only we were not so tired. But as the crests
toppled over and revealed the rays of the setting sun
through their emerald sides, the sight was one to gladden
salt-weary eyes.

There was more and more wind, and in spite of the
reef in our mainsail, *Wilful* was hard pressed at times,
driving her rather lean bow into most of the seas so that
the water swept over her foredeck, rising in cascades
over the fore-hatch and round the mast. Yet what seemed
a glorious slicing motion when one was steering became
a maddening series of jarring plunges during the watch
below.

The sunset on the second day out was a riot of colour —but a haunting livid blaze that boded no good. We were off the *Royal Sovereign* and the sky beyond the distant downs rose in streaks of pale yellow, deepening to orange in fleecy fragments of clouds whose edges, near the horizon, were tipped with silver and gold. It was a grand sight, but I did not like it. The sea was still big, and when I hove-to during my watch to put up the sidelights for the night, it was as much as I could do to keep my feet on the slippery deck. A Rye drifter came steaming down wind, her smoke racing ahead of her, while her high bow rose and fell with marked solemnity; and a rusty tramp, bound down the Channel, plunged on into the gathering gloom, lifting tons of white water over her fo'c'sle head and plunging deep, while her propeller churned up silver spray, and her smoke trailed low over her wake.

At midnight, when we had stood out far into the Channel and the lights of Beachy Head were only just visible over the tumbling horizon, the mate took over the tiller for her unenviable watch while I stumbled down the vertical companion and fell into the still warm berth all standing, to go off at last into a fitful sleep through sheer exhaustion. I was awakened by a tremendous crash, a shivering of the whole vessel and a dash of water into the saloon through the skylight. That must have been a steep one. But as I lay against the canvas dodger that keeps one in the bunk, the little vessel staggered up a long slope, lay over at a horrible angle, while spray clattered about the deck, and descended with another tremendous crash into the hollow, shivering from stem to stern.

Thoroughly awake now, I staggered up the companion

and was aghast at the conditions raging outside. The seas seemed to have grown to twice their previous size, the wind nearly tore my hair off and *Wilful* was labouring along with her lee-deck buried.

'Great Heavens, we must take some of the canvas off her!' I cried. Then I noticed the mate was steering from the lee-side of the cockpit.

'It's easier to be sick this way,' she said weakly.

We put *Wilful* about, stowed the staysail, while she did her best to shake us off her slippery foredeck, and rolled a second reef in the mainsail. When it was over I took stock of the situation. It was nearly two o'clock, the glass had dropped a further two-tenths, it was now blowing very hard indeed, the ebb was about done and six hours' flood would just about keep us pegging level in these big seas, the mate was sick and nearly done in; I was half dead from want of sleep and food and it would, at this rate, take us probably another twenty hours or more to beat up to the lee of the Wight.

Far away to starboard Beachy Head light showed between the crests driving past.

'We'll square away for Newhaven—and a rest.'

The mate nodded and eased off the straining mainsheet. Then began a sail that I shall long remember. Gone the short plunges, the up-and-down motion; in its stead a wild rush through the howling night, lifting bodily over great black beam seas that collided with our wash and drove in clattering spume across the deck and into our mainsail, while we tumbled bodily down their backs with the end of our boom dipping into them as we rolled. Water broke aboard forward, amidships, splashed over the quarter, and ran into the hurrying, hissing torrent along the lee-deck.

161

Down on the bottom of the well with her sou'wester against my knee, the mate dozed out of the wind, occasionally stirring to look through the lee-shrouds at the approaching light on Beachy Head. It was not blotted out so frequently now, but we still had some fifteen miles to go.

Ablaze with twinkling lights like a distant seaside town, a big liner swept across our bow, bound home to England. She looked as though she were riding as steadily as a train, as she would be. But it was too dark to discern the mass behind the rows of lights.

The sky changed from velvet to slate grey; paled in the east; clouds took shape; here and there a star winked dimly. The dawn had come. And with it, the seas became individuals and revealed their immensity. No longer hidden in gloom, their sides were grey and forbidding, steeper than I had imagined Channel seas could be, their crests curling over and roaring above the howl of the wind.

And still *Wilful* staggered, lurched, fell bodily, on, on, on.

The dawn strengthened. Far away off the bowsprit end we could now make out the lights of Newhaven, winking over the rolling waste of waters, maintaining an unequal struggle against the advancing day.

One by one they went out, and soon we could see the white cliffs and the little lighthouse on the end of the Mole. And *Wilful*, buoyant, aggressive, dominant, smashed through and over the seas, driving as I had never seen her sail before, like a mad thing. And when the day came, it brought with it a gale with scurrying grey masses of cloud that were reflected in the grey deserted waste of waters that raced madly up Channel.

At six o'clock we rushed into the shelter behind the friendly breakwater and swept up the narrow harbour between the piers into a haven of peace and calm and little cat's-paws; and when the deputy harbour-master clambered down to the staging and helped us make fast to a barge, he endeared himself to us by saying:

'My word, you must have had a night of it! You'll want to turn in for a few hours. I'll send someone to collect the dues at ten, not before.'

.   .   .   .   .

Newhaven is one of those few places which one can only leave after a struggle—unless there is a strong gale from about south by east blowing a swell straight up the harbour, when the railway station is the best way out. While we were there Newhaven was in a tranquil and demoralizing mood, and we indulged all the joys of giving ourselves up to its insidious effect for three whole days.

The sun shone, and under the lee of the high land enclosing the harbour it was warm and enervating, and we continued to nudge shoulders sleepily with the friendly barge, deep laden with cement, whose skipper told me they were also bound Spitheadwards, and had run in the previous night with the seas waist-deep over the hatches amidships. One dollop, he said, nearly carried the mate from the wheel.

There were jobs to be done aboard *Wilful*, and a coat of varnish had to be given the bowsprit, forehatch, the waterbreaker and even round the mast a foot up from the deck, for every atom of varnish had been scoured off from these places by the salt water.

In response to a telegram, my mother, who was to

163

have joined us at goodness-knows-what port down Devon-way for the second week of our holidays, came down and joined ship. It is her lasting regret that she was introduced to sailing just thirty years too late—when past fifty and in youthful tore-outs at that! After such early experiences, boats like *Wilful* appear to her to possess all the qualities and comforts of a steamship.

The wind continued to blow from the south-west, but *Wilful* began to show signs of impatience by chewing up a fend-off, while even the indolent ease of lying in harbour began to pall on us. All thoughts of being able to leave the boat down West had by now gone by the board and a few days' 'real yachting' in the Solent, to show the newly joined stewardess some of the popular anchorages, seemed to be all we could hope for. The barge skipper shook his head when he saw our preparations for putting to sea again, and told us he warn't goin' till 'e gort a fair slawnt, it weren't wuth it. I said we wanted to go west and our little ship was built for windward work, but he only mournfully remarked that it didn't 'ardly seem *fair* on the two leddies; 'e didn't approve of leddies bein' aboard bowts, anyway. Which almost made one of the two ladies flare up and advise the bargee to carry out an impossible operation on his head, but the stewardess managed to suppress the wrath.

We slipped out at three o'clock, past the long stone breakwater into a sunlit sea of emerald waves and sparkling crests. There was still a stiff south-west wind blowing and for the first watch we carried a reef in the mainsail as we stood off shore on the starboard tack, lunging and scending once more and tipping the crests with our bowsprit. Mothersill—the old remedy—appeared to be doing its work and the cheery stewardess

164

was quite happy sitting in the lee of the rather cramped cockpit.

At the change of the watches at 8 p.m., when *Wilful* was some fifteen miles off Brighton, the reef in the mainsail was shaken out in order to drive the boat a little harder, and we were soon washing the varnish off the deck fittings up forward once again. The sunset was not too depressing and the glass had risen a tenth, but with night came a shroud of fine mist, chill and clammy, which drove past and blotted out the stars and the distant shore lights. Into a thick murkiness, with the rays from our sidelights appearing like luminous phantoms of red and green against the white pall of the mist, we plunged on, sending out showers of spray from the lee-bow that were tinged for an instant with blood as they leapt past the port side-light.

At some sleepy hour in the early morning during my watch, when the night was ageing but the coming day was not yet suspected, I became dully fascinated with a constellation of three stars that appeared just above the horizon under the lee-bow. Their brightness surely foretold the lifting of the mist and I began to speculate on a clear dawn when it occurred to me that stars rarely appear in bright colours, such as red, green, and yellow.

I bore up hurriedly and went close round the stern of the deep-laden tramp steamer that burst forth out of the gloom and drove past into the night with a rhythmic rumble of her engines and a soft washing of the seas against her bluff bow. A door opened under her bridge and the figure of a man stood for an instant silhouetted against the orange rectangle. Then it shut with a clang, and as we passed through the subdued medley of her wake a smell came down wind to us, a smell that it like none other on earth—the delicious haunting smell of a steamer, of coal and galley smoke, hot oil, steam and smoothly running engines and a scent that comes from all ships that work for a living. Then she was gone into the night and *Wilful* lifted her head and plunged on.

By eight o'clock in the morning, when I took over for my next watch, we had the Owers light-vessel close abeam. The wind had taken off considerably during the previous watch, and now we were making very slow progress against a lumpy head sea with the main boom lifting and shaking all the wind out of the mainsail. By making a long board out from The Park off Bognor, we had hoped to take this south-west wind on the beam and to go romping up to Spithead on the last of the ebb.

It was a mistake. If I had watched the barometer more carefully and been on deck to notice the falling off of the wind I might have known there was to be a break, and we could have slipped through the Looe Channel. We had no sooner gone about for the long reach down to the Wight than the wind fell away, became fitful and exasperating, and veered to the north-west.

Tired as we were to the point of weariness of turning to windward, and only too eager for the anticipated beam wind up to the shelter of the Wight, this sudden shift of wind again in our teeth appeared to us as though some malevolent force had been at work and had fiendishly enjoyed watching our long tack out past the Owers, merely to throw the wind in our faces like so much contemptuous dust.

In spite of the warm sun and the fine weather we turned up the next twenty miles with regrettable phrases on our lips which became empty and meaningless by the
166

time we fetched up the narrow entrance to Wootton Creek in the evening sunshine and let go in the sheltered pool with the hum of insects filling our ears. The resigned contentment of the stewardess, who regarded a long beat of some twenty-six hours to windward in the clean, pure air of the Channel far better than the heat of a town on such a summer's day, had put to shame our own voluble impatience. Never again, we secretly told ourselves smugly in our new-found salvation, never again would we find abusive fault with the winds of heaven; here was peace, a calm anchorage with the trees and greensward at Fishbourne close by, and from now onward we would encounter contrary winds with a set grin of pious satisfaction at our immunity from exasperation.

That we broke these pretty vows on the first occasion only goes to show that not only were restricted holidays never intended for virtuous people, but the title of this story is well earned.

Two whole days were spent in sailing about the Solent to such places as Beaulieu, Yarmouth and Cowes, where many fine yachts were admired. The sight of these beautiful and luxurious craft lying off the old town brought up the evergreen discussion on what we should do if we had great wealth. I confess it would be a harassing problem to me that would undoubtedly banish all happiness and contentment, but perhaps I should buy or build a big yacht—a really big yacht—to satisfy one latent desire which would, perhaps, then become a wonderful possibility. I should want a vessel large enough to allow me to have aboard a full string orchestra.

But the mate pointed out that my ideas in more ways than one were inclined to run on the lines of an Eastern potentate!

During those two days our old enemy the south-west wind had returned with fresh vigour, and on the evening of the second day we rushed into Cowes with a reef in our mainsail and our decks glistening with the wet of a Solent popple.

An idea occurred to me.

'We're all sick of fighting this south-west wind. Let's make it our ally, set the squaresail, and go for a jolly fine run non-stop back to Harwich or even Lowestoft. We'll start to-morrow morning!'

The mate and stewardess were enthusiastic, for, truth to tell, we were already tired of pottering about the Mecca of yachtsmen. We hurried ashore just before the shops closed and laid in fresh provisions, then, aboard again, made all preparations for going to sea, as the sun set in a blaze of departed glory beyond the dark hills. The deep-sea dinghy painter was shackled on, the stern drag warp brought aboard, spars lashed down on deck, the cowl ventilator replaced by a screw deadlight, the biscuit jar, fruit and water bottle stowed in one of the well lockers for the benefit of the helmsman, the squaresail bent and got ready for hoisting, and so on. We took the Scout motto really to heart.

And next morning, when for once we got up when we said we would, and started to get under way, the south-west wind was nowhere to be found. The following gale, the blustering, shouting wind that had tried us sorely for days, almost driven us crazy with nervous disappointment; the fair breeze that was to send us scurrying ecstatically up Channel, praising the ship, delighting in the bellying, straining squaresail and the hurrying wake; the incessant wind that would drive the green, heaving seas after us and lift us forward with

168

'*WILFUL* LAY . . . LOOKING SILENTLY AT HER OWN
REFLECTION'

each roaring, frolicsome crest, that very commotion for which we now waited, was gone.

In its place was a stark, glassy calm. So still that when we drifted out into the Roads *Wilful* lay quite motionless, looking silently at her own reflection. So we drifted down Spithead, scowling at the sky in the west for signs of the jeering breeze that had hidden itself.

'Are we to spend the remaining few days left to us drifting in sight of this unholy land?' we cried, in impotent wrath from the sun-scorched deck. 'Can it be possible that this calm will last? Surely the wind, the south-west wind, will come again!'

None of us would consider renouncing the idea of a run back to home waters, and thus, when the first few cat's-paws scurried timidly across the water from the high land of the island and gently caressed our mainsail, so that the mainsheet withdrew its folds from the water and the drips fell from it and kissed the rippled surface, we trickled on past No Man's Fort, the Warren and the Nab End, pointing our bowsprit in the direction of the Owers.

The wind fell away and left us becalmed; came again in little puffs, flirted with our tired burgee and slowly, oh, so slowly that it left us speechless, the land of the Wight dropped astern and night closed around us, while the stars came out, one by one, and looked down sorrowfully at themselves twinkling in the water. With drooping mainsheet and idle headsails, *Wilful* rolled to the ground swell, occasionally hurling her boom to the limit of its tether, jerking the four-fold sheet into the air amid a shower of tinkling water drops. Again a little breeze came up astern, the tiller stirred, and *Wilful* began to take heed. But during the three hot days in

171

Newhaven, and the days in the Solent, her bottom had developed a growth of weed that caused her to be sluggish and unlike her beautiful old self in these pestilent fickle airs.

Daybreak found us becalmed, with our gear slamming and rattling, a quarter of a mile past the Owers. The ebb had hold of us now, and *Wilful* began to soak stern first down towards the light-vessel. The ignominy was too much for our proud ship, and I felt 'the time had come' to start the engine, the first time, incidentally, since our racking experience on the Knock John sand. In *Wilful* the Kelvin is installed in a separate small engine-room behind a door which is just abaft the main companion. In hot weather, with the engine running, this compartment, which was originally a single-berth cabin and extends under the self-draining well floor aft to the transom, becomes like a greenhouse. When we had been running for two hours, therefore, and the engine stopped on account of a choked paraffin pipe, the task of cleaning this—during my watch below— was such a distasteful one that we let the yacht drift while the engine-room cooled down a little.

But the sun scorched our necks and the deck burnt our feet; a faint westerly breeze rippled the water about nine o'clock and we made a few miles with the spinnaker drawing limply and the weed on our hull waving in the deep green water. The heat shimmered on the sea and the white cliffs of Newhaven, which came slowly abeam during the afternoon, appeared like a mirage far away to port, so far that it was only with the binoculars that we could make out the breakwater and its minute light-house standing like an upright cigarette end at the foot of the cliffs.

Rippling the water, first in uncertain patches, then as far as the shaded eye could reach, the breeze followed us and filled the spinnaker; the dinghy lifted its painter clear of the water and chuckled after us as we approached Beachy Head, and in the cool of the evening, when we had miraculously brought Bexhill abeam, the little breeze died and left us wallowing once more, lifting the trailing weed on our hull out of the water as we rolled with a trickling sound. The sun tipped the horizon, a red ball without a cloud to be seen, and no sign of any coming wind in the sky. Tired beyond words of this clattering of gear and idle drifting, we started the engine and brought up, as darkness closed in, as close under the stone break-water of the little fishing harbour at Hastings as the fall of the tide would allow.

With the anchor down, we could all three turn in for a night's sleep, but even this was withheld from us in part. The swell continued and *Wilful* rose and fell, rolled and staggered as though she had gone mad. At times the port lights in her topsides were obscured as she nearly dipped her rail, and the anchor cable ground on the bobstay and snubbed with irregular savagery. And then, at four o'clock, a combined shouting mingled with the throb of a noisy motor, and followed by a crash alongside, brought me hurriedly through the forehatch to find a Hastings lugger rubbing our topsides. What on earth had happened? A collision? Why, our riding light still swung jerkily at the forestay, casting a baleful glow around. A hoarse voice, accompanied by a wet slab of something soft on deck under my nose, explained the matter. Did I want to buy a couple o' plaice and a nice small sole? Just in from a night's fishin'.

I confess that at that moment, as I stared sleepily at

173

the mess of slimy fish before me and the clumsy lugger ground her tarry side against *Wilful's* white enamel, I cursed the Channel and everything in it from the depths of a tormented soul, and felt that if the elements would only let me get my ship back to the friendly old sands and swatchways, withies and creeks of the Thames Estuary, I would sell this deep-sea cruiser, even though she was the finest all-round small cruiser I have sailed aboard, and buy an old fisherman that would sit on the mud and give me peace—and a real holiday! Which, if I may digress, I did a little over a year later, and my friends who admired *Wilful* have never forgiven me, and much less been able to understand it! But that is another story—with a moral on Contentment.

At ten the next morning, in a blaze of relentless sunshine and a mirror-like calm, we started the engine and throbbed slowly through the shimmering haze towards Dungeness. The heat on deck was painful to our feet, while in the little engine-room it was like a stokehold in the tropics, which I was able to appreciate when compelled to clear the paraffin filter! For the sudden heat wave of 1928 which, for the benefit of the evening newspapers, broke many records, was upon us, and all we asked for was a secluded, tranquil creek in which to anchor, stop the incessant din of the motor and just enjoy the heat and bathe. Instead, we continued to grope our way to Dungeness, the most inhospitable, unsheltered spot one could imagine, and spend the night rolling at anchor close to the Newcome buoy.

And the next day, which was Sunday and the last day of my holiday, we slowly motored to a point a few miles off Folkestone, where the paraffin gave out and left us windless and helpless, drifting down Channel once more on the ebb in water almost too deep to anchor. It looked as though we were to spend yet a fourth night rolling at sea, but a 'sixpenny sick' from Folkestone, crammed with perspiring trippers, whose interest in our scanty attire was well expressed in the word 'Lumme!' came alongside, and, after tense haggling, sold us five gallons of paraffin at quite a reasonable price. We were thus able to motor into Dover Harbour just after dark.

I had to catch an early train next morning to face an accumulation of work, for it was close on Press day, while the stewardess reluctantly had to return home later, leaving the mate aboard the boat in the outer harbour. The next I heard of *Wilful* was a telephone message a few days later from the mate at Harwich, who had arrived there single-handed after a twenty-hour passage from Dover, during which a fierce squall at daybreak had split the mainsail right across and given her a nasty hour or so to windward of the Sunk Sand! But that, as the newspapers would put it, is 'an exclusive story.'

XI

The Enchantment of the Sands

THE ebb was almost finished now and, soon, the young flood would be filling that fascinating net-work of little creeks that lay between us and the London River.

We had enjoyed our gentle drift down the winding river from Fambridge before the fluky cat's-paws, and were now brought up off Burnham water-front in the pleasant sunshine of this Sunday afternoon, while the other small yachts which had accompanied us proceeded down the river towards Shore Ends showing distant in the slight haze.

They would have to be back on the flood to catch the evening train to London, while we were bound through the creeks to the Kentish river with half of our summer holiday to play with. Contented and unhurried, with the lordly air of time-worn bargees, we had let go our anchor, leaving the mainsail set, restless above our heads, while the ebb ran itself out and allowed us to gaze at the coming and going of craft from the familiar anchorage.

The breeze was now steady, blowing soft and warm like milk across the Essex pastures from the west, and when two hours later we paid off before it, the boomed staysail bellying out bravely like an embryo spinnaker and the scarlet streamer fluttering at the masthead, we

176

felt compassion on the crowd of small craft returning now from Shore Ends on the first of the flood. For us a week's delightful philandering amid the places we both love was only beginning.

Between the banks of the Roach River, where the wind gusts sent invisible finger-tips scurrying through the long grass, we made short boards and blessed the docile staysail that looked after itself. Into the narrow little creek between Foulness and Potton Islands we thrust our way, just able to lay our course, while our wash followed us along the muddy fringe of the banks which, ere long, would be covered by the in-creeping tide.

The silence of the place, broken only by the gentle rustle of our progress and the crackle of the aftermath on the shore, was already taking its magic effect on me. These creeks, with their stillness and solitude, were once more exercising their charm and making me more than glad I had bought back this old boat to explore them once more.

Against the blue skyline on the top of the Foulness wall twenty-one horses were standing in a row of uncanny precision, beautiful Army beasts whose tails told of an active vendetta with the fly tribe. I counted them again and again, never quite sure of the number, until the mate drew my attention.

'Don't shove us on the putty,' he said.

When we came to the entrance to the Narrow Gut that leads past Havengore Island to the lifting bridge, I felt that *Storm* was sailing in shallow water. She was. For fifty yards astern of us was a troubled streak of brown water, and even as I looked the tiller became dead and the dinghy ran up slowly and banged the transom.

'We're a bit before our time,' I said, as I lowered the staysail. 'The flood's only just making here, and there isn't more than 3 ft. of water anywhere yet.'

The mate knocked his pipe out on the mainsheet horse and grinned.

'Well, it's just half-past four,' he said, 'time and a good opportunity for tea.'

While I stowed the sails loosely and put the anchor over the bow, he had the Primus going, and by the time the tea-cloth had been hung up to dry and the cups and plates put back in their locker, *Storm* had swung to the flood and the banks were already covering.

The red sun was approaching the tree-tops behind Barling village, while above them, silhouetted against the sky, a group of barges' sprits and topmasts told where the quay lay beyond the meadows. With our mainsail scandalized and our staysail set we drifted quietly up the well-named Narrow Gut, our boom-end at times almost over the mud to leeward. Half a mile before we reached it the lifting bridge was raised while a couple of impatient cars kept each other company on one side of the gap, while more cars and bicycles were approaching along the dusty road from Foulness.

As we rustled through the narrow passage between the piers the bridge-keeper was already lowering the iron structure.

'How much water on the bar this morning's tide, Jim?' I called out.

'Three foot three inches, sir.'

The mate glanced back as he stowed the staysail.

'Shall we go out to-night?' and he nodded towards the thin line of yellow that lay between us and the distant ships that could be seen leaving the London River.

'It depends if the tides make any,' I said. '*Storm* draws exactly three-foot-three, so we may have to wait here for another tide.'

I rounded up and ran her forefoot on to the sandy horse below the bridge, while we stowed the sails and went off to sound for the deepest spot, for if we were to spend the night here we should want to sit upright when the creek dried out. Then we floated the docile little boat and let go the anchor. The distant bar was just beginning to cover with a sound like the soughing of the wind, and by the time we had had a dip in the warm water the flood, which we had brought with us, had changed its direction and was flowing in from the sea, causing *Storm* to turn round and face seaward again.

There was still plenty of time, for high water was at 10.2, according to Jim Cork's tide-table.

'Well, sir,' he said, glancing at his tide-gauge on the side of the bridge when we stood yarning with him, 'the tides has only just started to make, but with the wind drawin' out of the nor'-west as it is, it'll perhaps put this one up an inch or two.'

We had to be thankful for small mercies. An inch or two would suffice, for there was no swell. The last time I had been through here was also in *Storm*, when I had first owned her in 1924, and then we had had to wait two tides to get over the bar. We leaned on the parapet, which vibrated as the cars rushed past on their way home, and watched the water flowing in over the bar half a mile away, while far beyond a barque was running out into the gathering night, probably a split-wood ship bound for a Baltic port.

Storm rolled slightly in the middle of the creek. Built

179

originally for a Southend owner on bawley lines, she was almost the ideal cruiser for the Thames Estuary, and had endeared herself to me to such an extent that when I was forced to part with her six years before in unhappy circumstances, I swore I would buy her back. And I did, but not until I had owned and rejected three different boats in the meantime! To be ideal for this coast for me she would just have to be larger. As it is, her shallow draught of 3¼ ft. is a constant joy, especially as it still allows her, with her shapely hull, even though she has 9 ft. beam, to go to windward better than many deeper craft, while there is no obstreperous centre-board to cause leaks and other troubles.

At half-past nine Jim looked over at his tide-gauge, squinted at the bar, scarcely visible in the twilight, and remarked:

'There's just three and a quarter feet on the bar now, sir. The flood'll run for half an hour, so you might get over.'

That was enough. Within five minutes we were away, our mainsail squared off before the light nor'-westerly breeze. The sand-banks on each side slipped by slowly and it seemed a long time before we brought the line of little black buoys abeam.

The mate, elbows on cabin-top, pulled restlessly at an asthmatic pipe.

'Mighty slow progress this,' he observed as the first of the little can-buoys trickled past. 'How about a bit of engine?'

But I was in no mood to desecrate the eeriness of the place with the chugging of the motor. The whispering wind was urging us surely over the last indraught of the tide and we were nearly over the bar now.

'Take a sounding.'

The mate handled the sounding-pole, marked precisely in feet and inches, and looked concerned.

'Only three-foot-six.'

Yes, we were nearly over the bar. Here, looming ahead and just beyond the last of the buoys, was the old beacon that is the very devil to pick up when you approach from seaward. I do not know whether it marks the site of the original Orwell beacon which is shown in very old maps of these strange parts, marking the end of a spit at the mouth of what was then called Wakering Haven. You can see it in an old map of the Thames Estuary made by one Waghenaer in the year of the Spanish Armada. From this triangular spit, or 'gore,' comes the name Havengore, by which we know this place as it is now.

But that beacon, called Orwell beacon, is far from the river or ancient town of that name. That lies buried far to the north, beyond the Wallet. But if you go to the British Museum and look at these old maps you will see that not only did a channel run in across the Maplins, between what was then called the Black Taile and the Whittaker, but it branched outside the Haven and led north through the Wallot Deep, and so to the mouth of the Orwell. Thus this beacon led the way it was possible for shoal vessels to take in those days from the London River to the Orwell. When the north wind raged there would, I like to think, be many a clumsy billyboy riding to her hempen cable in the shelter of Wakering Haven. Since then the sands, even the very coastline, have changed. . . .

'Three-feet-four. Look here, old man, we'll touch presently.'

For a moment as we glided on it seemed we ought to touch with only an inch under our keel, for it had gone ten o'clock now and the ebb had just set in. But, no; as the breeze, warm and scent-laden, freshened slightly, *Storm* heeled gently and let the hard, level sand slip past from under her without so much as a 'scrunch.'

'We're over the bar. Now we've got three miles to sail across these sands before we can find water to lie in for the night.'

Three miles of smooth, yellow sand, which in a few hours would be laid bare like a desert. What a wonderful place this Estuary is! Somewhere in the dark away to port lies an amazing roadway, a mere track, attributed to the Romans, I believe. In a straight line leading from Wakering Stairs across the Maplins to the north shore on Foulness, with a sign-post standing gauntly out of the sands miles off shore, it is marked by rows of little besoms, or mapples.

When the tide is low one may walk warily along its four or five miles of length. Warily I say, for there are countless pools or linns along its pitted surface. These mapples marking the broom-way across the linns of the sands, surely this accounts for the strange name of the Maplins!

A stronger breeze came now, and little wavelets were turning over with flashes of phosphorescence, while our wake streaked astern like the Milky Way. In the cosy cabin the table was laid for supper, the table-cloth a rectangle of white above the crimson of the carpet, and the mate was attacking a hearty meal. While the boat sailed herself with helm pegged I sounded at intervals or sat on the bitts forward and watched the flashing wave at the bow. Four feet, five feet, five and a half.

182

For two miles there was not a fathom, so flat are these magic sands. Away across our starboard bow the lights of Sheerness winked dimly, while between them red, green and white lights moved constantly—the unceasing traffic of London River.

By eleven o'clock the white occulting light of the South Shoebury buoy was abeam, and I found five fathoms. Rounding up, I let go and stowed the sails to wait for the morning's flood up river. And with her riding-light dipping a pale gleam around her and the glare of the South Shoebury buoy a cable's length astern, *Storm* rode through the night while the dark, restless water washed past her bows away into the North Sea. . . .

   .   .   .   .   .

Towards the end of our week's holiday we passed this spot again, sailing hard with a fine northerly wind. Our days had been pleasant, for we had visited many of the old anchorages that we had not seen for two or three years—Hole Haven, Gravesend, Queenboro', Chatham and Stangate Creek. The still night in Stangate Creek, miles from civilization it seemed, when a full moon arose and we rowed silently round the little black cutter, while from my gramophone in the well came the beautiful intricacies of Tschaikowsky's *Romeo and Juliet* overture and other lovely things, will live in my memory. It is for nights like this that a boat has the right setting.

But to-day we were scurrying north along the edge of the Maplins bound back to West Mersea, hanging doggedly on to the tail of a friend's white 10-ton cutter which had come out of the Medway and had closed upon us with a cheery greeting off Shoeburyness. She also, it seemed, was bound for Mersea Quarters and for some miles had done her best to shake us off. But *Storm* was holding on half a cable astern like a terrier after a sheep-dog, thoroughly enjoying the impromptu race.

The ebb had nearly done by the time the Maplin light was a mile away on our starboard beam, and we were creeping in as close as we dared across the sands, for the wind was drawing a little more easterly.

With his 6 ft. draught my friend was wisely keeping out of the shoal water, and was now nearly a mile out on our starboard beam; but it was, for him, a longer way round.

There is a pronounced bay inside the spidery-looking lighthouse, with about 4 ft. of water in it at low water. In olden times there used to be a definite channel which ran through at this point into the Wallet at the place where the Spitway now divides the Buxey from the Gunfleet. Then also there was a long sand outside which bore the ancient name Goenfleete and gave the present sands their name.

'The wind's drawing right ahead and taking off!'

The mate's indignant voice brought me back to the present, and I found we were pointing out towards the first black buoy in the Swin.

The wind suddenly fell away, leaving us lobbing about in a short jump. This was too bad, for we still had to get to the Whittaker beacon, a mere matchstick four miles away, and the flood would begin to run against us at any moment.

Almost as suddenly as it had dropped, the wind came in from seaward, from almost due east, bringing with it cold spray as *Storm* lunged ahead with her lee-rail awash.

The white cutter was smashing into the short seas,

heading out into the middle of the Swin. The flood was running against us now and the Swin Middle light-float had turned to it for some time. While our rival made long boards towards the East Barrow Sands and back we kept over the Foulness shoals, cheating the tide and holding our own in the slacker water against the bigger boat's superior windward qualities against the seas.

It was a hard tussle to weather the end of the Whit-taker, and when we made a cable's length to leeward of the beacon after a long board, I decided to risk crossing the spit over a little swatchway—a mere undulation in the sands—I happened to know.

The seas had got up rapidly and several were breaking over the shoal part, and it seemed foolish to risk hitting the hard bottom on a lee-shore, but I trusted to finding this little swatchway, and bore up. With sheets eased, *Storm* tore across amid a smother of broken crests.

'Only five foot here!'

The mate looked apprehensive for a moment, for he is used to 5-ft. draught, and took another rapid sounding.

'Fathom!'

We were over, thanks to our shallow draught, and running hard up the Whittaker Channel, while the white cutter was making a last board out against the strong tide in the Swin to give the beacon a quarter of a mile berth. We had to let go the dinghy's stern drag warp and veer the little boat to a 10-fathom painter, for it was blowing fairly hard now.

With the lead going, we cut half a mile inside the West Buxey buoy, in 4 ft., and hugged the Buxey edge close, for we were close-hauled now and I wanted to fetch across the Bachelor Spit in one board if possible.

We were cutting things very fine, for the boat became a little sluggish once and I noted a brown streak in our wake for 50 yards astern. Then our heel touched slightly once or twice; but it didn't matter, for there was no sea here under the lee of the sands. By now my friend's cutter was over two miles astern, running up the Whittaker with his peak eased, for his boat is a little hardmouthed. It would be touch and (maybe) stop in the Rays'n, for there was barely 6 ft. there yet. Perhaps it was only to give us a run for our money that he chose our course, instead on going the longer but deeper way through the Wallet Spitway.

Across the Bachelor Spit in a little over 4 ft. again we bore up and squared away for the Quarters, having managed to save, in all, some six or seven miles' sailing by being able to take such short-cuts.

As the wind died and darkness closed in we drifted, calm and contented with our passage from Hole Haven, past the drunken old Nass beacon, past the familiar old withies waving in the tideway, right up Thornfleet creek to bring up close to a fine old oyster smack.

It was nearly an hour later that the white cutter stole in and let go her anchor lower down in the Quarters.

Storm, a thorough little Essex cruiser, had done all the things she had set out to do.

XII

With 'Juanita' to the 'Other Side'

THE mournful tolling of the bell-buoy at the mouth of the harbour, a spasmodic cacophonous din as the iron cage rose and fell on the uneasy swell that gurgled past its weedy sides, reflected the feeling of depression which had descended upon me.

The ebb-tide, pouring in a vast oily stream out of Harwich Harbour, carried *Juanita* with it, while her sails flapped aimlessly in the calm evening air, and as we drifted out past Landguard Point into the well-named Rolling Ground, I sat with the lifeless tiller in one hand and thought how foolish it was to start on a long passage across the North Sea in a flat calm with a yacht that has no engine when we might have been anchored up a quiet creek away from everywhere, listening in content-ment to the tide leaving the mud.

But it was not for me to complain, for I had given my promise that this year I would spend my summer holiday as crew aboard my wife's yawl and go for a jolly cruise across to Holland and back.

Believe me, it was not done easily, this little business of convincing me that I should enjoy a cruise in deep water for a change, even in such a fine, little deep-water packet as *Juanita*. I pointed out that I never felt really happy inside when at sea for long in a small yacht;

187

that I'd much prefer to go for a pleasant cruise, say, to the Kentish coast and the Medway, and spend each night at a different but peaceful anchorage; that I had been working very hard and was feeling run down and in need of a *quiet* holiday free from worries, business or domestic. I reminded my skipper that I had only just recovered from the deplorable effects of a septic throat and knew I ought to have as restful a time as possible. You notice how each argument became more desperate as the previous one failed?

It was no use.

'You've *never* had a cruise of any length aboard my ship,' Peter had replied, 'and I've crewed *your* various boats every holiday for the last four years without complaining. Can't you come and enjoy a deep-sea passage aboard *Juanita* this year? It'll be a change.'

A cruise to a foreign country, to fresh places, I was assured, would do me good; the passage across the North Sea could be done, with a fair wind, in twenty hours; I needn't do more than just stand my watches, and I should simply love Holland once I got there; and in any case, my wife clinched the argument, we couldn't use my own 12-tonner *Afrina* just now, because she was in the shipwright's hands undergoing some repairs to her rigging.

And thus, on a calm, murky evening that in itself was a disgrace to the month of June in England, *Juanita* drifted out past the Rolling Ground, being swept by degrees towards the Cork light-vessel, bound for Flushing, with a hundred miles of treacherous sea to cross.

This was the fourth year that my wife had owned *Juanita*. A deep Falmouth-built yawl of 7 tons, high bowed with a fairly long counter stern, she has a reputation for wonderful sea-going ability and an unhappy habit of finding the mud where you least expect to. But then she draws 6 ft., which, to my mind, is excessive on a length over all of 32 ft., waterline 26 ft. and a beam of 8.2 ft., and immerses too much wetted surface for moving in light airs.

Below decks she is a model of cosiness and comfort, reflecting in every fitting, in every crevice, corner and gadget, the untiring improvement and work put into her by her devoted owner during her four years of sole possession. The previous winter had seen a raised addition made to the after end of the cabin-top, rather like the driver's cab of a·locomotive (in fact, I was in disgrace for a whole day for merely fitting up a dummy whistle-cord inside!) which not only protected the well, but housed the electrically lighted chart table which fitted just in front of the helmsman. She is a remarkable ship in many ways.

As twilight descended over the sea, a light north-easterly breeze came from the land and allowed us, with topsail and mizen-stays'l added to the 'four lowers,' to make about 4 knots on our course for the Sunk light-vessel. The slight mist of the evening increased gradually, and when the lights of Felixstowe began to appear over our stern they were soon swallowed up in the whisps of fog that were beginning to blow across the water. Night, cold and clammy, descended upon us, blotting out everything but our immediate world. The sidelights were put up and the little green binnacle electric light switched on, so that the compass card swam in an eerie bowl of translucence.

The light north-easterly breeze continued during my watch until midnight, and *Juanita* sailed on through the

189

darkness, her jib shimmering with the phosphorescence of the lee bow wave, and little *Punch*, the 8-ft. dinghy, following in our glistening wake with a ghostly light parting at his stem.

Wisps of fog, blowing across our bows, became tinged with red and instantly changed to pale green like intangible spectral chameleons, as they scurried in front of our sidelights, hurrying away into the gloomy night, across the sea to some destination no one knows where. And at regular intervals I could hear the dismal moan of the fog-horn on the Sunk light-vessel from somewhere ahead, while less distinct came the four unearthly grunts of the Galloper light-ship diaphone, like the frenzied groans of a neolithic monster in its dying agony. Every now and then the hoarse voice of a steamer's syren broke across the wash of the water, faint and uncertain, for the steamer track was some miles beyond the Sunk light and we were approaching it slowly.

At midnight I gave eight clangs on the brass ship's bell that hung just inside the driver's cab, and soon a sleepy skipper appeared in the tall rectangle of the doorway, silhouetted against the soft light of the cabin. She came on deck buttoning up her oilskin, for the fog penetrated wool sweaters and turned everything damp with its icy breath.

'Wind's taking off a bit, isn't it?' she remarked, looking round the constricted limits of our little world. 'Listen to those damn steamers. It won't be much fun crossing their track if it keeps as thick as this.'

As she spoke, the whistles of three different steamers blew one after the other, followed by the long sonorous blast of a motor-ship—the ringing blast of compressed air which is so clear in comparison with the muffled note of a steam syren.

'There're a lot of them about,' murmured the skipper as she settled to her four-hour watch, 'I might have to call you.'

During my watch below, from twelve until four, the wind died and left us rolling sluggishly somewhere before dawn, still enveloped in the cold mist, with the syrens of steamers approaching and getting farther away on both sides of us. I went on deck about two o'clock and found the skipper peering apprehensively in the direction of a steamer whose approach was heralded at intervals of a minute by the deep roar of her syren.

I rang the ship's bell loudly at regular intervals, and by degrees the direction of the steamer's syren changed until she was abeam.

'Listen! You can just hear her.'

And there, somewhere in the night, we could just hear the thump of a half-exposed propeller and the wash of a steamer's bow wave.

The skipper drew a sigh of relief.

'A tramp in ballast, bound for the London River, I should think,' she said. 'But I wish to heaven this fog would clear!'

I stayed in the well with her for the rest of my watch, for the presence of these steamers, blundering along through the fog and only making their probable position known by spasmodic whistle-blasts, was not too restful to either the nerves or the imagination, and I sensed her need of companionship.

Gradually light appeared in the sky and the day was born, and with it came a faint breeze from east by north.

191

It was enough to keep our sails quiet, and *Juanita* gathered way slowly once more, but the direction of this footling breeze only just allowed us to lay our course close-hauled south-east for Flushing. It failed to blow away the fog, and although the sun appeared mistily through the gloom, like a ball of wool, all the morning it could not break through the pall that covered the North Sea.

The regular four grunts of the Galloper came abreast of us during the morning, and once we caught a faint glimpse of the light-vessel itself through an unexpected clear patch in the fog. Then it was gone, and slowly the sound of the diaphone dropped astern.

All day these conditions lasted. Close-hauled on the port tack with topsail and mizen staysail still added to the jib, staysail, mainsail and mizen, *Juanita* was making about three knots on a south-easterly course, while every now and then patches of flotsam drifted into view, slipped by and were swallowed up astern, pieces of wood, boxes, half-submerged baskets, patches of weed, a medley of halves of grapefruit—a steward had thrown them overboard from some passenger vessel probably after breakfast—looking clean and fresh in the clear green depth of the sea. We looked for them, for they were our only connexion with the outer world.

Every hour we worked out our supposed position on the chart by dead reckoning, estimating our speed—for we towed no log, which would have been useless at this rate of progress—and the changing set of the tides and marking the ship's position with a fountain-pen on the talc cover that was clamped over the chart board to protect the chart from wet.

There seemed to be nothing to do in one's watch

192

below. There was nothing to see beyond the quarter of a mile circle of heaving water around us and the bits of flotsam as they passed into view and disappeared again. The boredom of being at sea for days on end would be quite sufficient to suppress any desire I might entertain of sailing off to the South Sea Islands or taking one's dream-ship around the world. It would seem such a hopelessly unsatisfactory life to me, so aimless and so desperately miserable on the days and nights for long periods when the whole world is composed of your ship and the immediate spot of tumbling ocean in which you happen to be. I can fully understand the conviction held by the average landsman that people who go for world voyages in small yachts for pleasure are quite mad, fortunately in a harmless way which reflects on themselves alone.

At six o'clock in the evening, when we were nearly twenty-four hours out from Harwich and by dead reckoning should be about five miles north-west of the West Hinder light-vessel—swept by the flood-tide all the afternoon some twenty-five miles south of our course for Flushing—the breeze suddenly came in from due east, freshened, and slowly began to disperse the fog. Our mizen staysail and topsail had to be sent down, and *Juanita* heeled over until the water gurgled in her lee-scuppers.

We had sighted nothing after losing the light of the Sunk some eighteen hours previously, and now this sudden breeze made us anxious to get our exact position; for we were approaching a low-lying coast with sand-banks stretching from it like the Thames Estuary.

With the gradual clearing of the fog the sun appeared and we found ourselves sailing hard over a sea glistening

193

with white wave-crests, *sailing* for the first time on this passage.

'There's the West Hinder!'

The skipper handed me the binoculars, and I could make out through our lee-rigging the three masts and topmark above the horizon.

'Well, that's settled our estimated position as correct,' she said, 'but it means we're about twenty-five miles to leeward of our course and we can't lay any higher than this. This wind's heading us off from Flushing. Shall we go for Ostend for the night? We can just about lay it.'

Peter drew her finger across the chart to the alluring name of Ostend, and I breathed thankfully the magic words, 'Let's spend to-night in Ostend.'

Out of a clear, hard sky the easterly wind freshened still more, and soon we had to shorten canvas again. The jib was rolled up with the Wykeham Martin furling gear, and while we hove-to the skipper had ten minutes' struggle with slatting canvas on the after-deck, stowing the mizen. The seas were increasing in size and *Juanita* was bucking and plunging, throwing out fountains of rainbow-hued spray from her lee-bow.

This is where one sees the chief advantage of this yawl rig of *Juanita's*, when canvas has to be shortened at sea or in a hurry. Putting two reefs in the mainsail of my 12-ton smack and changing to the No. 2 jib is an exhausting labour fraught with desperate hauling on reef tackles and slipping about wet decks, whereas in *Juanita* the jib is rolled up from the well and the mizen stowed—a matter of only a few minutes at most—and there you are snugly rigged and perfectly balanced under main and staysail, with all your canvas inboard.

194

Under way once more it seemed but a matter of a few hours before we should be entering the peaceful calm of Ostend Harbour. The wind was steadily freshening and the horizon to windward had a steely, clear-cut look about it that suggested much more to come.

'We ought to fetch the piers soon after sundown,' remarked the skipper, burying her face in the collar of her oilskin as a dash of spray splashed against her sou'wester.

The thought of getting into port was comforting, for we had neither of us had more than an hour's sleep since we had left Harwich, and meals had gone by the board, for both our insides were decidedly 'uncertain.' The strain of the anxiety of the previous night and the hours of exasperation during the day when we knew we were being carried pitilessly miles to leeward of our course with a useless and tantalizing wind gradually heading us off, were beginning to tell on us. I was heartily sick of this uncomfortable lumping aimlessly about in the North Sea and yearned for a secluded creek and a quiet anchorage for the night and, above all things, a complete rest.

But the sun, a fiery orange ball with rays of yellow radiating from it, sank below the distant land, and still we were at sea with the low Belgian coast just visible through the lee-rigging.

'It's all we can do to lay up to Ostend on this tack,' Peter said grimly.

I did not answer. I already had misgivings, for I had been working out the tides in my head, and it seemed to me the flood would turn against us in a couple of hours' time.

We passed one of those tall pillar-like whistle-buoys

that are used on this side of the North Sea, and its hooting sounded hollow and forlorn out there in the twilight. It was as though the thing was laughing at us as we plunged on our way, smashing the seas with our powerful bow and filling our lee-deck with water.

Slowly we closed in with the barren coast, and when the lights began to appear one by one my heart sank. For there, far away on the *weather* bow, was the triple flash of Ostend high light, at least eight miles to windward of us, while a foul tide was just beginning to run its six-hour spell against us.

A couple of Ostend fishing-boats, fine high-bowed ketches puffing along with their single cylinder semi-Diesel engines, passed us close and their crews shouted at us, but their words were carried away on the wind. Our hope of making the harbour for the night had vanished, and we sailed close in to the beach at Middel-kerke, a desolate-looking little place six miles south from Ostend, hoping to find the Roads smooth enough to let us anchor. I do not think I have ever felt so utterly tired, and the craving for rest and peace for just a few hours was intolerable.

But there was to be no rest. The wind was blowing along the shore, allowing no shelter, and had we dared to anchor the yacht would have put her bows under and probably parted her anchor cable.

'We can't anchor and we can't heave-to and let the ship take care of herself,' I said bitterly, 'for we might get foul of any of those channel buoys. Besides, we should lose ten miles with this tide running if we did. There's nothing for it but to go on beating all night until the tide slackens!'

What a tragic realization that seemed to be—to have

to admit that after hoping for hours to be in harbour to-night we should have to go on sailing for the next six hours merely to hold our ground against this relentless tide! Not merely sailing, but banging about with such a violent motion that the man off duty had to hold on to keep from being thrown across the well. Neither of us could stand the cabin now.

We had had no food for over eight hours, for the skipper had already been sick and I was on the miserable verge several times, but after a strong tot of neat whisky we both felt stronger and less depressed. And so during the hours of darkness we thrashed away doggedly into some of the steepest breaking seas I have ever encountered, drenched with heavy spray, our decks full, our bows occasionally swept and, several times as a sea hit them and tossed the ship's head up as we came about in stays, the long counter was buried. What a night that was, and how tantalizing were those cheerful red and green lights on the ends of the harbour piers a few miles away!

When dawn came and the tide eased off, we had made the six weary miles to the whistle-buoy off Ostend. Here we hove-to while I broke out the red ensign at the masthead and coiled down the tangle of halliards which a heavy sea had swept into the lee-scuppers.

Then with *Punch* towing heavily half-full on the end of a long painter we bore up and staggered through the seas sweeping across the entrance between the piers and carried our way into the subdued swell under their shelter. As we sailed slowly up the long harbour the sudden quiet and calm seemed too wonderful to be real, and we perforce had to look astern and watch a local fishing-boat reeling drunkenly towards the entrance, the

197

spray driving across her in sheets, to realize that the wind had not suddenly dropped.

With his engine puffing vigorously the tough-looking fisherman drew abreast and waved his arm up the harbour.

'I tow you to the yacht anchorage?'

We shook our heads. Old *Juanita* would do it with a little coaxing, and both of us like to manœuvre wherever we want to under sail alone if possible. And so, as the town first began to show signs of life at this early hour of five in the morning, we let go our anchor off the yacht club-house, thirty-five hours out of Harwich.

No one came to worry us and we were able to indulge in a few hours' luxurious sleep that drew a veil over our miseries of the preceding night. The wind flew into the south-west, and for three days blew great guns, piling up a big sea outside that dashed against the outer piers and blew across the harbour entrance in drifts of spume.

Life was pleasant here, for there was plenty to amuse us on shore, and we found the fishing harbour full of fascinating craft and interesting characters. We liked the custom of painting their vessels' topmasts and spars in bright colours, orange, white and red, blue with white rings, green and yellow and so on, while these bold-looking ketches, all of them with heavy semi-Diesel engines installed below hatches, looked clean and well cared for. Except for their size, they were very similar to my own smack which I had left at Pin Mill, and I then and there decided that I would paint my topmast a bright colour when I got back.

On the fourth day the south-westerly gale had gone down and left a nice, fair wind for Flushing. It tempted

198

us out of the harbour soon after dawn to catch the tide that would be turning to the north.

A suction dredger was moored across the middle between the piers at the entrance, and with our sails blanketed by the quays and a big swell rolling up the harbour, *Juanita* plunged and tossed, shaking what puffs of wind that came to us out of her sails and threatening to drift down on to the anchored dredger.

But a stronger puff filled our frantic sails, held them steady for a short time and just took us clear into the open sea, and we began to breathe again.

Outside a vile irregular swell was rolling in from seaward, the aftermath of the two days' gale, and when the following breeze began to fall off about eight o'clock, as we had dreaded it might, *Juanita* was rolling her main boom into the sea, gybing the mizen back and forth and lifting fountains of spray as the mainsheet fell into the water and then tautened with a thud. It was only by lashing a preventer guy to the lee-shrouds that we were able to keep the boom comparatively quiet.

Peter's face was a study.

'God, what a climate!' she almost screamed. 'Either a blasted gale or a flat calm! Just look at this swell!'

But it *was* maddening to lie becalmed and helpless now two miles off Zeebrugge when there had been too much wind for three days; and the motion of the boat, pitching, lurching, reeling and twisting, with the continual rattle and clatter of sheets and blocks, was anything but soothing to tired nerves. Then it began to rain, to pour in torrents for an hour, and we took refuge in the cabin.

'I'll be as sick as a cat if I stop in here,' said my poor skipper after a few minutes, and braved the downpour

199

on deck, looking like a disgusted young seal as she stood hunched up in her glistening oilskins.

Our fair tide was spent and soon we found the low, sandy coast, with its odd groups of stark, stone houses, like teeth that have been planted in a row in the sand, beginning to slip past the wrong way.

I took a cast of the lead—three fathoms—and showed how it streamed out ahead. We were definitely drifting back towards Ostend.

'The flood's beginning,' I said unnecessarily, as I coiled the dripping lead-line into its box on deck.

The skipper glared at the receding shore a mile away and darted a look at the sky—the kind of look a woman would give a successful rival in a love affair.

'All right. *Let* go then. I suppose we'll roll our insides out here for the rest of the day!'

The rattle of the cable through the fairlead drowned the pithy comments that followed on the weather, and particularly the kind always meted out to us when she and I go for our summer-holiday cruise together. I knew from experience it would do her good to 'have a good swear,' and the most tactful thing for me to do was to keep busy on the foredeck. By the time I had stowed the dripping sails and gone below I found her gnashing her teeth by way of crunching biscuits, and it was not difficult by then to bring back a twinkle into her eyes through the mundane agency of a cup of hot tea and some buttered toast!

The rain ceased its steady downpour and became drops that tinkled on the water round us and pattered irregularly on the cabin-top. Then it ceased altogether, and like a smile appearing on a care-worn face, the sun broke through the clouds and turned the oily grey sea into jade green. Presently, too, a little ruffled patch appeared here and there, coming towards us across the water by devious ways, as though timid and uncertain of approach. The little cat's-paws brought the beginnings of a breeze from astern that made our burgee flutter hopefully at the masthead, and *Punch* awoke to life and whispered to his parent ship.

'There's enough breeze to stem this flood now.'

I loosed the mainsail tiers and began to winch in the anchor cable. Soon we were under way again with a smart breeze, leaving astern of us a long wake of scintillating lace-work on the surface of the waves.

Far ahead we could just see the great gaunt electric crane that stands in the shipyard at Flushing—or Vlissingen, as it is known—and dominates the town. That crane is the landmark of Vlissingen, just as the tall church spire marks the little Zeeland town of Zierikzee; as the high, white lighthouse, like a cigarette on end, leads the mariner towards Ostend—long before the houses can be seen—and the famous 'stump' dominates Boston in Lincolnshire for miles around. The windmills of the Netherlands are almost all gone, and in their place are harsh iron-works, cranes and power cables.

Towards six o'clock in the evening we had entered the mouth of the Scheldt, rolling in with a smart breeze and a steep sea overtaking us, and were soon carrying our way inside the outer harbour. Three very short tacks brought us to the lock gates, where warps were taken and made fast, and *Juanita* came to rest in the lock.

The skipper had just time to change into beautifully creased flannels, reefer jacket and a cheese cutter pressed on at a perky angle before Officialdom requested the

201

'Captain' to step ashore with the ship's papers and the crew's passports. Left in charge, I busied myself in stowing and coiling down, and ere long the skipper returned with the documentary evidence of her complete ownership, and we were let through to tie up alongside the piles on the port hand just inside the canal.

Here we were at last at Flushing, and here we stayed for four days while the weather grew intensely hot and we discovered how enervating the place can be. There was plenty to do—there always is aboard a sea-going ship—and we put in several hours varnishing the rails and hatches, whipping frayed ropes' ends and splicing new strops. The incessant rolling of our passage across from Harwich and round from Ostend had caused a great deal of chafe which had to be seen to.

Flushing was disappointing this time, for the water in the canal was 6 ft. below its normal level, owing to repairs to a bridge farther up, and it needed an acrobatic feat to get up on the wooden gangway along the piles from one's deck, while the water itself was thick, stagnant and smelly.

On shore the chief nuisance was the children. Oh those Dutch brats! I confess I have never been able to worship at the shrine of 'The Kiddies' of any age, and the shrieking hordes that could never get accustomed to the skipper's flannel trousers could not have guessed how near they came sometimes to being murdered in pairs. ... But in Holland the stolid Dutch parents make a religion of their offspring, stay wisely indoors and discharge the mobs into the streets to find amusement there, to the exasperation of the visiting foreigner.

There are no cheerful little cafés open nearly all night as in France and Belgium, while the only restaurant we went to about nine o'clock, hoping for a really good meal, told us they did not serve dinner after seven-thirty and hinted that it was already ten minutes past their bed time!

There were two other English yachts in the canal, one, a 12-tonner with a family aboard, had been there, we were told, a month. We wondered how they could stand it. The other, a small cruiser-racing yacht, was owned by a handsome clean-shaven yachtsman in spotless attire, who reminded me so much of the drawing of a yachts-man going ashore in a dinghy in a well-known advertise-ment that we always alluded to him as 'Players Please.'

Torn between the need to rest and the desire to take the first opportunity to slip out through the lock and make a quick and joyous passage home to England, we continued this unfortunate holiday at Flushing. But the summer of 1931 had gone mad, and was as fickle and dangerous as a hornet that has just landed on a hot brick.

Just how joyous our passage back home was to be is a story that is reserved for the next chapter.

XIII

The North Sea Gale

M Y holiday was drawing to a close and we were
by now anxious to get a fair slant of wind back
home. One day it was calm, sultry and blazing
hot, the next a fresh south-westerly gale piled up a sea
outside and drenched the little motor pilot-cutters as
they went out to put the Scheldt pilots aboard incoming
steamers.

But we decided we could not stay tied up in this dull
place indefinitely, and on Saturday morning of June 13
we locked out at midday and drifted into the Scheldt
at high water in hot sunshine, hoping for a breeze. All
the previous day it had been blowing hard from south-
west, and as our course for Harwich would be north-
west a breeze from the old quarter would serve us well
and perhaps give us at last a fast and enjoyable passage.

But the usual luck which dogs my meanderings on
holiday again followed us, and when the breeze came it
was faint and fickle from north-west, just dead in our
teeth. Peter took it as quite to be expected—'I don't
think we'll ever get any reasonable weather again' was
her comment—but I felt irritated and vexed at our con-
sistently bad choice in the matter of winds. Was it
possible that we should *never* be blessed with a fair wind
on a long passage?

'Look at that! Isn't that the last straw?'

The skipper's tragic voice brought me to my senses and I saw, coming in with this breeze from the sea, a thick bank of fog, its clammy hands already clutching at Flushing, a mile away, and enveloping the town in its dense folds. A fickle head wind and now—fog! Just the conditions we had encountered coming across, only *this* time, because we were hoping to get back, it had decided to blow the other way.

There was no time to lose. The land at the mouth of the Scheldt was being blotted out from view, and we had only just time to take cross bearings of Breskens lighthouse and the harbour and the land just left before we found ourselves enveloped in the chilly driving mist, while the sun paled and became a dim ball of fluff in the sky.

'Trying to beat out through the Deurloo channel in this stuff is out of the question,' Peter said resignedly; 'it's quite hopeless to expect to drift about in the North Sea indefinitely with all this traffic about.'

Even as she spoke three or four steamers coming down the Scheldt started to give vent to their own dismay with doleful solos on their syrens. 'What the devil *are* we to do?'

'Make a fair wind of it back to Ostend,' was my suggestion, and it was accepted.

We made one board right into the land on the Belgian side of the Scheldt and caught sight of the Nieuwe Sluis lighthouse dimly through the mist, coming about close in to the beach; another board on the port tack allowed us to fetch one of the black buoys off Flushing which suddenly appeared under our lee.

Then we were able to square away a little on the starboard tack up the Wielingen channel along the coast for Ostend. Except for the lighthouse and the black buoy we had sighted nothing, although we could trace the approximate movements of one or two steamers that were entering and leaving the Scheldt by this Wielingen channel by the sound of their whistles.

It was uncanny to be sailing along quietly out there in that utter void for hour after hour, seeing nothing but a patch of grey water two hundred yards around us, and beyond, above, everywhere, nothing but the pale impenetrable grey of the fog, yet to be able to mark off on the chart our estimated position at the end of each hour.

Once, while I was peering through the lee-rigging, the mist seemed to take shape, and my heart missed a beat as the shape darkened, formed, grew into a mass and became a big, deep-laden tramp steamer that blundered into our vision a hundred yards away, slid past with a faint wash of water at her bluff bow, and was swallowed up in the fog astern without another sound! Soon after a powerful tug appeared just as silently with a tow-rope that stretched away into the fog. Then presently its tow came into view—a huge steel lighter of the Rheinschiff variety fully a cable's length astern of the tug!

We rang our bell after that at fairly regular intervals, for it was not too comforting to think that there may be other steamers lumbering along this same channel without a single warning from their syrens.

About tea-time we picked up the sound of the Zeebrugge fog-horn, three short agonized howls, a pause, and then a fourth gasp, repeated over and over again as it slowly drew abeam and, as the evening advanced, trailed away into the fog astern. Soon the fog-bell at

Blankenberghe came faintly to us. That, too, was slipping by.

'We've got the tide with us now.'

Although we had still seen nothing of the land and sighted no buoys since leaving the Scheldt, we knew exactly what the ride was doing to us by the *Nautical Almanack* and the book of *Tidal Streams* which the skipper had been referring to. About seven o'clock she came into the well and marked our estimated position on the chart, some five miles from Ostend, two miles off the coast.

'We ought to see Ostend piers in an hour's time,' she said in a matter-of-fact, damn-you-Mr.-Mate-I'm-skipper-aboard-this-ship kind of voice, 'Call me if there's any change,' and disappeared below. Peter is practical to the point of exactitude when it comes to navigation, and sure enough, at eight o'clock, the ends of the harbour piers at Ostend showed through a lifting fog a mile off our bowsprit end, the first land we had seen for nearly eight hours.

It happened that at the same moment that we saw the piers we also caught sight of one of the Dover–Ostend packet-boats approaching from the west and do her spectacular turn about half a mile from the pier-heads, to enter stern first. It did not look as though there would be room for both of us, but as the tide would sweep us past the piers and make it impossible to get back if we dallied about outside, we went straight in, followed by the steamer, which looked a great mass towering above us. The jetty took the wind out of our sails and we rolled in the swell with virtually no steerage way, but the rows of port-holes of the *Prinses Astrid* slid by harmlessly within a few feet of our boom end and we drifted into the agitated water closing round her bow, to follow her wake up the harbour. It was one of those horrid moments you encounter in artificial harbours.

By nine o'clock we were anchored in our old berth off the yacht club. It was Saturday night and we were tempted to take a tram into the town for one last good dinner at our favourite restaurant, but decided that as it was necessary for us to start the next day for Harwich if the wind was at all possible, for I had to fill an editorial chair in London on Tuesday at the latest, a large dinner was not a wise thing to take to sea.

The next morning, to our amazement, was not only fine, but about eleven o'clock a nice south-easterly breeze sprang up as well. A following wind for home! It seemed too good to be real.

'Do you know the glass has dropped *six and a half tenths* since last evening?'

The skipper's incredulous voice did not impress me.

'Well, it's only come down to normal, more or less,' I replied airily. 'It was 30.3—a silly height for it to be —and now it's simply 29.65. We can't let a *fair wind* go to waste, can we?'

At midday we left the pier-heads and sailed out upon a sunny sea speckled here and there with little glistening wave-caps. The wind was dead astern and we set our topsail to make the best of it. Conditions could scarcely be better; the sky was blue, if a trifle misty, and the sun bright, if a wee bit pale; while this lovely breeze was warm and cheering, driving us on our way at a nice five knots.

'This will be the first time you and I have ever had a fair wind on a long passage together,' I said as I went below to prepare some tea. It was then twenty-five minutes past four and Ostend was now out of sight astern some twenty-two miles. I was reaching for the methylated bottle to light the Primus . . .

'I say, come on deck.' There was something in the skipper's voice that made me leave the Primus and go out into the well. 'Have you ever seen clouds like that before?'

The wind had suddenly fallen away, leaving us jumping about in a somewhat lumpy swell that was coming in from the west. In the same direction I saw several vicious milky clouds with drooping fingers so low that they seemed to touch the funnel of a tramp-steamer that was a mile to the westward of us. They were hurrying towards us at an uncanny rate. A peculiar haze had enshrouded the sun, and the whole sea had suddenly lost its brilliance and sparkle, as a smiling face will change and blanche at a terrifying sight.

'Why it looks almost like a hurricane sky,' I said. 'Look at that steamer's smoke!'

The steamer was listing towards us and the smoke from her funnel was being blown down in our direction, while a line of dark water flecked with white raced ahead of it.

'There's a devil of a squall coming; you'd better clew up the mizen while I stow the jib!'

I had just rolled up the jib and turned to lend a hand to Peter who was struggling with the mizen, when the wind came. Amidst a shriek that tore past one's ears and seemed to loosen the hair of one's head, *Juanita* lay down and wallowed, her lee-deck buried, with water lapping over the coamings into the well, while spray flew over her weather rail and thudded into the straining mainsail. Peter was manfully trying to muzzle the flogging mizen with one arm round the mast which lay over at some fifty degrees. I was unable to go to her assistance, for I had remembered that the topsail was still aloft, and when I looked up the canvas was beginning to come away from the bolt rope. It would not stand the strain for long, while it was almost burying the ship.

As soon as I started the sheet and halliard that rag of sail went mad. It was impossible to stand anywhere on deck and I had to sit with one leg each side of the mast. It was as well, for the topsail at once became a raging kite, blew to leeward of the lee-rigging, and lifted me up so that I had to grip the mast with both knees. Then it swung back with a crash against the gaff and caught on the peak halliard. I was able to ease off the halliard a little more then without being pulled up the mast before hauling savagely on the down-haul, and gradually the topsail spent its energy and came down, to be immediately drenched with spray, disentangled from its ropes and finally rolled up, a sodden mass, and pushed on to the well floor.

By this time Peter had stowed the mizen.

'Get the staysail sheet aweather!' She must have shouted in my ear, but I only just heard her. 'We must get her hove-to.'

With the clew of the staysail just to weather of the mast—it took the two of us to get it there—*Juanita* lay hove-to, but still on her beam ends, quite overpowered, while she drove into the seas, burying her whipping bowsprit. From the well the skipper was pointing at something with a grim look on her face. Then I saw why. The mainsail luff rope had parted half-way up.

There was nothing else to do but haul the mainsail

210

down, a wicked job with the slippery deck gone mad under one's feet; but when it was stowed *Juanita* felt easier and surprised us by lying safely hove-to under her *staysail* only. We eased the clew to the mast to give the sail a fair flow and lashed the helm down; then we took stock of our position.

'Thank Heaven that staysail's heavy canvas with good manila sheets,' breathed the skipper, and then was overcome with sea-sickness. I wedged myself in the well, protected from the flying spray by the 'driver's cab,' amazed at the fury and suddenness of this gale. Here we were hove-to under the minimum of canvas just over twenty miles off the Belgian coast when a quarter of an hour earlier we had been sailing gaily over a calm sunlit sea with scarcely a cloud in the sky! I sat there drenched, feeling cold and awe-struck at the growing majesty of the elements, the roaring wind and the great green seas that, in an incredibly short time, mounted up and came towering upon us to pass away to leeward with broad, foam-flecked backs hissing and growling. I still felt bewildered and stared at the chart under its talc cover, weighing up our position. The flood was running southwest, almost against this wind which was coming from a point south-of-west; we were lying between northwest and north-west by north, and, strangely enough, making about 1 knot through the water on the latter course. Provided this gale did not veer to north-west and provided our gear stood, we should be able to lie like this even when the ebb should start to carry us to leeward. But let the wind veer to north-west and we should have the terrible shoals of the Scheldt estuary twenty miles under our lee . . .

Juanita, deep, game little Falmouth yawl, had come

into her own and I was filled with admiration for her. She was behaving wonderfully, lifting her high bows stubbornly to the great seas, taking the shocks with a shudder as an occasional monster broke on to her weather bow with a crash of thunder, throwing the spray right over her and filling her lee-deck, and then plunging wildly down the steep back, tossing her counter stern high and sending the water cascading forward down the lee-deck to meet the next lot coming over the bow. . . .

The motion was almost incredible. These seas were as big and high as any I had ever seen in a gale in the Channel, but they were steeper, more inclined to curl over and break than any Channel waves. That is what made them so difficult for any boat to negotiate. *Juanita* was hurled rather than lifted, and nowhere could one get the slightest degree of comfort or rest. The cabin was in hopeless disorder, the mattress and cushions of the weather berth having piled themselves on to the floor, while the lee-berth was occupied by the movable table.

My poor little skipper had long since passed out and was helplessly sick over the lee-coaming of the well. I decided to make an attempt to straighten the ship below, lash the table to the 'windward side and so clear the lee-berth for her to lie on, but a few seconds in the wildly-pitching cabin were enough to send me lurching back into the well to pay my own tribute to rollicking old Neptune. . . .

Afterwards I felt better and rushed into the cabin again to re-stow the mattress, the cushions, the table. Ah, that table was a curse, and I had to pay three hurried visits to the lee-coaming in the depths of utter misery

'"JUANITA" HAD COME INTO HER OWN'

and back again before I had the lee-berth clear. Then I
helped Peter below and tucked her up with a basin to
gaze at, and hurried out again to collapse in a corner of
the well.

For a time I watched, dully fascinated, the antics of
Punch on the end of his long painter. The little dinghy
was already half-full and it seemed impossible for him
to rise to some of the seas that swept past our stern.
Yet for a long time his green-painted bow appeared over
the top of each crest and swept down the back of the
sea until our own stern was lifted high in the air to blot
the sight out. Then at last a huge roaring comber hit
Juanita a blow on her side, filled her decks, smothering
her, and broke completely over little *Punch*. The next I
saw of him the dinghy was floating with his stem and
gunwale just above the water, waterlogged and lifeless.

Never in my life have I felt worse than I did then.
The gale had increased and the seas were becoming so
majestic as they bore down on us that I preferred to
watch their backs slipping away to leeward. As we rose
to the crest of a mighty hill I took a look round the
horizon, but there was nothing in sight except a waste
of heaving grey backs and glistening snow-white crests.
The North Sea seemed deserted. Somewhere ahead, a
few miles, was the Hinder Bank, which with only 3 or
4 fathoms over it would be causing a terrible and dangerous sea, and we were slowly forging ahead towards
it. . . .

The evening wore on and the sun began to near the
tumbling horizon, but still there was no sign of the gale
abating as quickly as it had sprung up. The seas as they
approached us, wallowing in the trough, reared their
heads between us and the sun and revealed in glorious

translucent flashes of green, deep and mysterious, the transparency of their forms. For a long time I sat in the well, holding on to the weather coaming, fascinated by these ruthless monsters and the wonderful way in which the little vessel negotiated them, then I felt I could stand it no longer, and went into the cabin to collapse on the floor, too sick and exhausted to do anything.

'Oh God, when will this ease off?'

The skipper's agonized voice was dreadful to hear.

'It'll go down with the sun.'

I said that, wearily; but the sun was by now tipping the horizon, it was nearly half-past nine and there was no sign of any abatement. Supposing, I thought wildly, this hell was going on all night, where should we be driven to in the darkness? We were enduring, as I learned by Meteorological report later for this area of the North Sea, a Force 8 gale attaining Force 9 at times, a wind velocity of 45 to 50 miles an hour. Little did we think that during this time the French pleasure steamer *St. Philibert* was overwhelmed near Ushant and nearly five hundred passengers drowned, and that at Birmingham this same gale developed into a tornado and wrecked buildings and damaged a great deal of property. And this in the merry month of June!

The misery continued, and lying on the wildly-bucking floor of the cabin, listening to the thunderous crashes of the seas on our weather bow and the swish and gurgle of the bilge water beneath the floor-boards, I thought of the various accounts I had read (yes, and published in the *Yachting Monthly*) of yachtsmen who had lain hove-to in small yachts in 'the Bay' or off Land's End or the North Atlantic and their descriptions of how joyful it was to have no work to do but to lie, in one's bunk, smoking, reading and eating (eating, ugh!) while 'the little ship looked after herself.' I suppose if one could avoid being seasick and were sure of plenty of sea room and not such short, steep seas, conditions would be easier and one would soon get used to it. Certainly I had not minded thrashing down Channel some years previously in a friend's 20-tonner close-reefed in the teeth of a summer gale. The seas had merely been longer and more regular.

At last, as twilight descended, the motion became less violent; *Juanita* rode more easily and seas no longer broke against her weather bow. I went on deck and found the wind still blowing hard, but not so fiercely. The sun had disappeared now and all round us were moving hills and gloomy hollows with here and there a white, roaring crest. Away to leeward was the loom of the North Hinder light, and when we rose to the top of a sea, about four miles to windward I could just see the West Hinder light-vessel itself, silhouetted against the heaving skyline.

I decided to try to set the mainsail and get the ship under way, for I knew we should both feel better when she was sailing once more. I put the suggestion to the skipper, who weakly agreed to have her ship under way again. But I advised her to stay in her bunk for a time.

Hauling on the halliards with a slippery deck lurching wildly beneath one was no joke, and I was feeling nearly exhausted from the five hours' ordeal of chronic sickness. But in due course I was able to crawl aft, trim the sheets and sail the ship, and soon the skipper came out into the well and sat huddled up against my knees. A tot of whisky and a few digestive biscuits made us

217

feel better, and all night we took it in watches to drive the little vessel close-hauled on her north-westerly course for home. She went slowly, for she had the drag of the waterlogged dinghy astern.

Dawn—like all the dawns I have seen at sea—was cold and cheerless, and when the sun appeared it was lemon-coloured and metallic. To our dismay the wind had veered a little more to the north-west during the night and we were only able to lay north-northwest, which brought us miles to the northward of the Galloper light-vessel, thirty-five miles from the English coast. The wind was increasing again steadily with the strengthening of daylight and the seas were once more preposterous and vile for sailing. Every now and then a comber reared up, and do what one could with the helm, it would break on to our bow, drive in sheets into the mainsail, drench and blind us, and leave *Juanita* with all way stopped and her decks full to the rail. Then she would stagger onward once more, lying over and taking it green along her lee-deck.

It was about half-past four that I felt the ship was sailing faster. Then I looked astern and saw why.

'Pete, *Punch* has gone!'

The skipper roused herself from her corner in the well and looked sorrowfully at the frayed end of the new 2-in. bass towing painter. It was no use sailing back, for we should never be able to see a submerged dinghy in such a sea. Poor Peter, she was particularly fond of *Punch*, and we never saw the little boat again.

All the morning we drove the trembling little yawl through that horrible sea, both of us weary to the point of exhaustion, the realization that now that the wind had gone more into the north-west we could not pos-

218

sibly fetch Harwich, sinking cruelly into our tired brains. About ten o'clock we sighted England and the Shipwash light-vessel, and at two o'clock in the afternoon we crossed the north end of the Whiting Bank and closed in with Orfordness, the gale, having driven us fifteen miles north of Harwich, still blowing with unabated fury.

But here it was slightly off the shore, and as the ebb had now turned against us and we could not even make a yard against it we ran round the Ness and let go the anchor close in to the beach to await the turn of the tide in four hours' time.

Oh, the joy of that anchorage, pitching wildly though we were! A wash in hot, fresh water, a mug of Bovril, biscuits and three hours' sleep, terminated by a ruthless alarm clock, put new life into us, and when we had to face a hard thrash dead to windward again at six o'clock —for, with ironic and consistent cruelty, having driven us here, the wind now backed to south-west, which would have allowed us to fetch Harwich if it had only done that earlier in the day!—we accepted this last onslaught against us as a matter of course. For five more hours we endured the old discomforts, the violent motion, the lunges and dashes of cold spray, all over again.

A clock from somewhere over the trees, black masses in the darkness, was striking the hour of midnight as *Juanita*, weather-beaten and weary, sailed slowly up the Orwell, the cold night wind caressing her sails gently now as an uncouth lover shows remorse for his savagery of a moment before. The familiar trickle of the dinghy was absent, and the little white yawl seemed to ghost with strange silence up the dark, placid river, feeling her way beneath the stars, a tired, bruised thing coming back home. . . .

The skipper opened the cabin door and let out a flood of yellow light, and I caught sight of a white table-cloth within and supper half laid.

'My God, what a passage!' she said. 'Thirty-six hours out from Ostend and the dinghy gone!' Then she closed the door behind her and I found her hand in mine.

'Glad to be back in your old river, mate man?'

I was. I tell you, I prefer these creeks and rivers and swatchways for *my* kind of cruising.

XIV

Changeable Weather

A S the old smack took her usual long sweep round
and brought the wind aft, the little town that we
were leaving looked as though it were still asleep
in the morning sunshine.

The white mixture of smoke and steam belching
forth in rhythmic puffs from a train pulling out of the
station was the only indication of life that we could
actually see.

Nearly twelve years had elapsed since Derek and I
had ruthlessly left Woodbridge behind and charged
down the river in my 2-ton *Dabchick* before a fierce
winter wind. With snow lying on the ground, Woodbridge had appeared inhospitable on that occasion. Since
then I had paid several visits up the delightful winding
Deben to the little town, each time, I verily believe, in
a different boat! But never had Woodbridge looked so
attractive, so unspoilt with its quaint old tide-mill and
its sea-wall and the houses rising over the hill beyond,
as it did on this bright August morning when we
weighed our anchor from the secluded little bay at
'Kison.'

The sun shone on the expanse of mud flats that were
rapidly being uncovered by the tide, and as we ran
down that aptly-named Troublesome Reach —for rarely
does the stranger navigate it without making the acquain-
tance of one or other of its shoal patches and tricky turns

—a soft westerly wind rustled the group of trees at the mouth of Martlesham Creek, where we had spent the night, and caused the long streamer at our masthead to flutter in a scarlet streak against the azure background of the sky.

I always covet that house that stands in its garden at Kison, a good square pile half hidden by trees, that peeps down the river nearly as far as Waldringfield. To live comfortably in a place like that, to have one's boat on moorings in the creek at the bottom of the garden, to keep a dog . . .

'We'll have to gybe soon.'

The mate's voice recalled me from my daydream and I walked aft to haul in the heavy mainsail. I had not owned *Afrina* long, but I had already learned that although a 12-ton smack-yacht can be sailed single-handed under ordinary conditions, there are times when she can be a handful even for two. Gybing in a fresh breeze is one of them, and there have been times when, being alone, I have run nearly a mile before being able to gybe.

Hauling in the 2-in. Manila mainsheet when a fresh breeze is filling the mainsail needs every ounce of one's strength, while the tiller has to be lashed and the boat made to sail herself. Then the weather runner has to be slacked off and the lee-runner braced up. Each needs quite a walk round the deck. Then a foot or so more in on the mainsheet and—crash! Over she comes, and you have to push the helm hard up with all your might to keep the boat from rounding up into the wind. For *Afrina*, unlike most boats of her type, is quick on her helm and needs careful steering.

For many years this old boat had earned some smack-man's living as a Colchester oyster dredger working out of Brightlingsea, then some yachtsman with an eye for a boat had bought her and converted her into a sturdy and homely, if not exactly a smart, yacht. She was a fine vessel for her size, measuring 35 ft. overall, 31 ft. on the water-line, 10 ft. 3 in. beam and but 4 ft. 6 in. draught. Full-bodied and comparatively shallow, she was just the type of boat that I liked, yet the antithesis of my wife's *Juanita*. She was roomy and cosy below, with a wide saloon which in cold weather was cheered by a coal stove, and a small separate sleeping cabin aft having two spring bunks, while one of her chief virtues, so useful on this coast, was that she would sit upright when aground. Like all boats of her type, she had an immense bowsprit, a 6-in. Oregon pine spar, standing 15 ft. beyond the straight stem, which put the fear of God into any yachtsman who thought of crossing our bows a little too close! I was proud of that bowsprit and kept it well scraped and varnished.

'The wind's freshening a bit,' said the mate as she stood, her feet wide apart with both hands on the long tiller.

It was true. A sudden gust filled the mainsail and caused the old ship to heel slightly, while the water turned over under her lee-bow with a gurgle that steadily grew into a joyous roar. Fleecy clouds were capering across the blue sky, looking almost as white as our bellying mainsail, while the wooded banks of the river on either side were slipping past at a fine rate.

By the time I had coiled all the halliards and catted the rusty 80-lb. anchor in the approved 'Brittlesea' fashion, Waldringfield—a tiny hamlet nestling amongst the trees on the west bank of the river—was passing. I waved a kiss to the mate and began to wash down the decks.

These were no white, spotless decks demanding the deference of soft shoes. They were solid decks painted with red ochre and linseed oil, giving them a restful deep-red colour, while the inside of the bulwarks was pale buff and the timber heads supporting them and the hatches in the deck were emerald green. This bright colour scheme suited the old vessel and she carried it off well, but I had not yet painted her topmast emerald green, too, as I had decided at Ostend.

'Will you take the helm a moment, skipper? I want to put my smock on.'

I took the tiller until the mate reappeared up the companion with her canvas fisherman's smock, which keeps the wind out better than three sweaters. Then I went forward again to lash down the dinghy, which we had stowed bottom upwards against the starboard rail. We carried it thus, for we were going to sea and might meet anything between here and, say, the Crouch.

After the exhausting holiday to Ostend and Flushing my wife and I had had in her yawl I had declared that the next few days' holiday I got would be spent idling up my beloved creeks and rivers in my own boat. And for two days *Afrina* had been doing it, but somehow the westerly wind and the ebb-tide had called to us both on this fine morning and we had prepared the ship for a passage round to Paglesham, in the Roach River, both anxious for a good sail with this sturdy old hooker beneath our feet. But we reckoned without the weather of 1931. . . .

Past the long horse—that treacherous middle ground which was already awash in the centre and is marked at

224

the upper end only by an absurd little, black buoy—the banks became shingle and closed in on either side, leading out past the chain ferry connecting Bawdsey on the north shore to Felixstowe Ferry on the south, over the bar into the North Sea. The tide was hurrying faster and faster now, hustling us through the narrows willy-nilly as we hauled in our sheets for the close-fetch down this last reach.

'Are you going to take a pilot?'

With her hair curling out from beneath her béret and her face wearing a grin of sheer joy, the mate nodded towards a collection of wooden bungalows and huts which formed Felixstowe Ferry. One of the local pilots was watching us through binoculars, but I did not dip our streamer.

'No. We came in without one and I'll risk it,' I said, taking over the helm.

Woodbridge Haven, as the entrance to the Deben is called, is not quite so treacherous as Orford Haven, although it has a nasty bar of shingle banks that, after an easterly gale, shift and hump up in unexpected places. This time there was a great bank of shingle, like a flat-topped necropolis, 5 ft. high above low-water mark, which formed a small channel to the north of the main one, and as we opened out the ugly-looking line of white crests and troubled water ahead, I could not help thinking of that winter's day Derek and I had nearly wrecked little *Dabchick* on this bar.

'Take a sounding.'

The mate swung the lead, which is kept coiled on deck for immediate use, and said: 'Five and a half feet.'

We were just over the bar on the shallowest part and

with a fair swell running could not have had more than a few inches to spare under our keel in the hollows. But we were safely over, a 6-knot ebb rushing us out past the little, black buoy. And the lead-line was recoiled and no comment made.

The fact is, after several years at this game of cruising, you begin to take it so seriously and the various experiences and frights make you so cautious that you become too darned efficient and sure of yourself. This necessary cautiousness and careful forethought against emergencies take away a great deal of the uncertainty and adventure which are ever present in one's first cruises. But after saving you for the first year of your yachting career the little cherub that looks after inexperienced sailors gets tired of you and leaves you to the mercies of old Neptune. He doesn't like people who make mistakes, the irascible old scoundrel, and adventure, like spring, is never far behind. . . .

The wind was in our teeth for the Naze, the cliffs of which were nearly 'hull down,' although the eternal Naze tower, which I am told was erected in 1720 as a landmark by Trinity House, was plainly visible. The ebb was not done yet and for an hour we thrashed away to windward without making much headway. Then when the Cork light-vessel had turned to the young flood the seas became steeper, and *Afrina* punched her powerful bows through their green faces so that they tumbled over the rail forward, closing over the bitts and the capstan as though trying to grasp the ship and hold her down. But always her black bows rose again and the infuriated water, foaming with rage, was bundled out through the lee-scuppers.

Harwich Harbour opened out away off our starboard

226

beam, and before long we were off Walton-on-the-Naze, with the tumbling waters of the Wallet before us.

'The wind's backing,' said the mate; 'we can't lay the Spitway buoy at all now.'

Her tone suggested deep resentment, for we had counted on making a good leg through the Wallet Spitway. I gave an absent-minded reply, for I was below in the saloon cutting ham and cucumber sandwiches.

'The wind's piping up out of this cloud, too,' she added later, with her mouth too full for words.

The wind certainly had freshened. We had just come about near the edge of the Gunfleet Sand, and *Afrina* was driving hard on the port tack with her lee-scuppers awash; every now and then a heavy lump of green water crashed over her weather bow, rushed along the lee-deck and filled the quarter-deck to the height of the rail, until it drained away through the scuppers. I took a long look at the sky to windward, for it appeared black and heavy and had already hidden the sun.

'I don't think we shall have to reef,' I said finally. 'It won't be more than a rain squall and we can just trice up the tack if necessary. Better go about.'

Afrina went round on to the other tack again with a clattering of canvas and several headlong pitches, then she was off, heeling well over to port and filling her deck with frenzied water. There was a good deal of water and spray about and we had by now donned our sea-boots and oilskins. The wind was whipping off the crests of the seas, and the spray that was hurled from her lee-bow was blown away to leeward in a mist that revealed the suggestion of a rainbow.

Then the wind came with a violent squall, a blinding deluge that drove into our straining mainsail with a loud hiss. *Afrina* lay over still more under the fearful strain, her decks full to the cabin-top, staggering under the dead weight of the water.

Suddenly a dull thud seemed to shake the whole ship. My beautiful bowsprit was bending like a bow.

'Shove her round on the other tack, the bowsprit shroud's carried away!'

'All right. Lee oh!'

Scarcely able to face the blast of blinding rain and stinging spindrift, we put the old ship round on to the port tack once more and hove her to with the staysail held aweather.

'We'll have to get the small jib set and put a couple of reefs in the mainsail,' I shouted into the mate's ear. 'Help me stow that jib!'

While we fought the terrific weight of wind in that big jib—it was our largest, or No. 1—*Afrina* lay hove-to, crashing her great bowsprit into the seas and lifting her head wildly as they surged under her, doing her best to throw us off the fore-deck. By degrees we had the maddened sail down, then with a terrific plunge of the ship it filled with water in a monstrous bag, tore itself loose from our hands, all but dragging us overboard, bellied out, and began to flog in the wind like an immense kite. In my haste to gather it in, for it might burst to ribbons at any moment, I let the outhaul slip through my fingers, but by our extra effort the jib was conquered and lay, like a deflated balloon, a sodden mass around the bitts. Then I had to clamber half-way along that wildly dipping bowsprit to retrieve that unspeakable outhaul with a boathook.

228

'WE FOUGHT THE WEIGHT OF WIND IN THAT BIG JIB'

229

We dragged the limp sail aft and stuffed it down the sailroom hatch in the after-deck. The tanned spitfire was hauled out and set on the bowsprit, then I staggered aft again, almost blinded by rain and spray and hauled down the second reef cringle with the tackle, using, it seemed, my last ounce of strength. When I turned round, panting, my shipmate was grimly tying in the reef pendants.

It was blowing harder than ever now, a full summer gale, and the rain was so thick that the cliffs at Frinton, half a mile away, were blotted out. When all the reef-points had been tied and we had swigged up the peak once more, I sat down on the weather rail and took stock of our position.

'Not much use trying to beat to the Crouch against this,' I bawled into her ear. 'Why, we'd have a hell of a dusting even to make the Colne, and with one of our bowsprit shrouds gone, Heaven knows what might carry away next. Better run for Harwich.'

We had to scandalize the mainsail—lower the peak and trice up the tack a little way—to keep the old ship under control as we bore up and steered a compass course for Harwich. Although Walton could not be a mile away no sign of the Naze was visible, and we tore along in a welter of rain, spray and howling wind, while the crests of the seas alternately lapped over our quarter-deck to run into the lee-scuppers, and roared level with our fore-deck as they raced us in our mad rush.

For a time I sat on the stem head facing aft, my ears filled with the song of the boiling water tumbling over at the bow, while aft I could see the mate, bracing herself in her sea-boots against the heeling of the ship, tugging at the tiller lines, her face almost hidden by the

231

collar of her oilskin. But her face wore a wide grin of exultation that said: 'To hell with the weather. This is *grand* sailing!'

While on the fore-deck I fished up with the boathook the bowsprit shroud which had carried away, and found that it was not the wire shroud which had parted, nor yet the hempen lanyard, but the shroud plate which had pulled clean out of the ship's side! As I bent over to feel what damage had been done, for the place was under water all the time, my fingers detected a hole in her side through which a bolt had been drawn, and it suddenly dawned on me that the water must be pouring in.

The sight that met my eyes as I pushed back the after-cabin hatch was shocking. The carpet in the saloon was floating in two inches of water over the floor-boards, several books had jumped out of the bookshelf and joined it, and a drawer under the port berth had fallen open and was *full* of sea-water, with some of my clothes floating in it.

I stuffed a rag in the hole in the bow, having to reach down into the hissing race of the bow wave to do so, then returned aft to pump the ship dry.

'We'll light the stove as soon as we get in,' I said ruefully, 'and dry all our things. Heavens, what a summer!'

Almost without warning the rain ceased, the wind eased off appreciably and the grey, heaving waters turned to sparkling green and flashing white as the sun suddenly broke through the clouds.

The storm cloud passed away to leeward, a black ominous mass, and as it went the land suddenly appeared through its grey skirt of rain, and soon the beach and promenade and the distant pier of Felixstowe had passed through the gloom into the sunshine, like a stage scene when the curtain is drawn aside.

Having set up the peak of the mainsail and hauled down the tack, I came aft and took the helm, bringing the ship's head round to port, so that her bowsprit pointed across the Pye Sands.

The mate looked puzzled.

'Aren't you going into Harwich?'

'No. Up to an old anchorage at the top of Hamford Water,' I explained. 'We can repair our shroud lanyard up there in peace.'

The wind, still blowing freshly but not so hard as in the squall, allowed us to fetch across the middle of the sands with a few inches under our keel, for the flood had been making for more than three hours now, into the channel that leads up between them and the Dovercourt shore. At Island Point, where the channel branches to port and continues a mile or so up to the Walton club house, we carried on up Hamford Water and let go our rusty anchor at the very top, close to my old anchorage which I had discovered in *Swan*.

Some hours later the mate and I stood at the end of a forgotten hard on the fringe of the little island called Horsey, looking in mute wonder up the tranquil Hamford Water towards the flaming sunset that was lighting up the whole of the sky. We held a loaf of bread and a can of fresh milk, for our visit to the solitary farm on this lonely island of pasture land, dykes and sea-walls, had been made to replenish our stores.

Neither spoke, for the wind had dropped and scarcely a breath came to ruffle the surface of the water. Old *Afrina* lay quiet at the head of the creek, her scarlet streamer hanging limp and the smoke from her stove chimney trailing upwards in growing spirals.

The sun sank lower. Far away behind us in the direction from which we had come we could just make out Dovercourt with its tall chimney and, beyond, the church of All Saints at Felixstowe, raised as by a mirage. Some two miles across these islands, towards the south, across the Wades that separates them from the mainland, the town of Walton was just visible; while towards the setting sun lay another mile of winding creeks and little sedge-covered islands with here and there a quaint group of trees, uninhabited stretches of wild, open scenery.

The hard was covered with several inches of soft, slippery mud and, wearing sea-boots, I swept the mate up in my arms and carried her down to the dinghy.

'Do you think the Vikings ever landed on this old hard,' she murmured, 'like this?'

We launched the dinghy and rowed quietly towards the old, homely smack, pausing on the oars occasionally to listen to the call of a redshank or a peewit from over the marshes, while the drips fell from the blades of the oars and made silent rings on the water.

'I don't wonder that you are fascinated by these wild places,' my shipmate remarked at last in an undertone, gazing about her. 'There's something mysterious about these deserted creeks and tiny islands that you never get in the Solent. There's probably not another living soul within miles of us, and yet just think of the crowds there must be hurrying home on the roads to-night. There's scarcely a sound, is there?'

I nodded towards our sturdy home, while the reflection of her mast, with its limp red pennant, inverted, quivered and writhed lazily in the water.

'Only one boat at a time *ought* to anchor in a place like this. A crowd would spoil the magic.'

'Yes, and the silence of these creeks,' she whispered.